# The Complete Slow Cooker Recipe Book UK

Easy & Authentic Slow Cooker Recipes That Will Surprise and Amaze Your Family and Friends

**Samantha Burrows**

© **Copyright 2022 - All Rights Reserved**

This document is geared towards providing exact and reliable information with regards to the topic and issue covered. The publication is sold with the idea that the publisher is not required to render accounting, officially permitted, or otherwise, qualified services. If advice is necessary, legal, or professional, a practiced individual in the profession should be ordered. -From a Declaration of Principles which was accepted and approved equally by a Committee of the American Bar Association and a Committee of Publishers and Associations. In no way is it legal to reproduce, duplicate, or transmit any part of this document in either electronic means or in printed format. Recording of this publication is strictly prohibited and any storage of this document is not allowed unless with written permission from the publisher.

All rights reserved. The information provided herein is stated to be truthful and consistent, in that any liability, in terms of inattention or otherwise, by any usage or abuse of any policies, processes, or directions contained within is the solitary and utter responsibility of the recipient reader.

Under no circumstances will any legal responsibility or blame be held against the publisher for any reparation, damages, or monetary loss due to the information herein, either directly or indirectly. Respective authors own all copyrights not held by the publisher.

The information herein is offered for informational purposes solely, and is universal as so. The presentation of the information is without contract or any type of guarantee assurance. The trademarks that are used are without any consent, and the publication of the trademark is without permission or backing by the trademark owner.

All trademarks and brands within this book are for clarifying purposes only and are the owned by the owners themselves, not affiliated with this document.

# Contents

| 1 | Introduction |
|---|---|
| 2 | Fundamentals of Ninja |
|   | 2-Basket Air Fryer |

What is Slow cooker? .................... 2
How to Use Your Slow Cooker ......... 2
Benefits of Using Slow Cooker ......... 3
What Can You Cook in a Slow Cooker? 3
Instructions for cooking: ............... 4
Cooking Tips and Warnings ........... 7
Frequently Asked Questions ........... 9

| 11 | 4-Week Diet Plan |
|---|---|

Week 1 ..................................... 11
Week 2 ..................................... 11
Week 3 ..................................... 12
Week 4 ..................................... 12

| 13 | Chapter 1 Breakfast |
|---|---|

Sweet Potato & Onion Casserole ...... 13
Hard-Boiled Eggs ........................ 13
Chicken-Apple Sausage ................ 14
Beet & Spinach Frittata ................ 14
Cinnamon Apple Pie Oats .............. 15

Cheese Veggie Frittata .................. 15
Mixed Berries Butter Toast ............. 16
Cheesy Oatmeal with Spinach ......... 16
Herbed Root Vegetable Hash .......... 17
Spicy Eggs in Purgatory ................ 17
Multi-Grain Granola with Cherries ... 18
Cheesy Omelet Casserole .............. 18
Hot Coconut Cereal ..................... 19
Apple and Granola Casserole .......... 19
Dates Millet Porridge ................... 20
Cranberries Quinoa-Oat Cereal ....... 20
Creamy Pumpkin Steel-Cut Oats ..... 21
Tropical Farro with Mango and Nuts ... 21
Nutty Granola with Dried Berries ..... 22
Healthy Vegetable Frittata ............. 22
Spinach Ham Quiche .................... 23

| 24 | Chapter 2 Vegetables and Sides |
|---|---|

Vegetable Broth .......................... 24
Veggie and Quinoa Casserole ......... 24
Easy Spaghetti Squash ................. 25
Beans Stuffed Sweet Potatoes ........ 25
Vegan Navy Beans with Cranberries ... 26

Healthy Beans ............................. 26
Cheesy Spring Vegetable Pasta ......... 27
Garlic, Spinach and Beans Chili ......... 27
Mashed Root Vegetables ................. 28
Udon Noodle Soup with Veggie ...... 28
Collard Greens with Bacon .............. 29
Onion & Bell Pepper Stuffed Tomatoes ...... 29
Cheesy Potato Gratin .................... 30
Roasted Vegetables ....................... 30
Roasted butternut Squash Purée ......... 31
Sweet & Sour Beets with Onions ...... 31
Herbed Greens with Onions ............ 32
Delicious Turkey Stuffed Peppers ...... 32
Garlicky Mashed Red Potatoes ......... 33
Bacon Cabbage Casserole ............... 33

## 34 | Chapter 3 Poultry

Chicken Veggie Broth .................... 34
Barbecued Chicken ....................... 34
Spicy Whole Chicken .................... 35
Herbed Chicken with White Bean Stew ..................................... 35
Healthy Salsa Chicken ................... 36
Thai Chicken Curry ...................... 36
Sweet Garlic Chicken and Carrots ...... 37
Chicken Strips with Tomatoes ......... 37
Spicy Chicken with Greens .............. 38

Roasted Fennel Chicken and Squash ... 38
Southwest Chicken with Zucchini ...... 39
Cheesy Salsa Chicken .................... 39
Chicken Noodle with Colorful Veggies ..................................... 40
Chicken Chili with Beans ............... 40
Sweet & Spicy Turkey Salad ............ 41
Garlicky Turkey Breasts ................. 41
Delicious Chicken Meatloaf ............ 42
Herbed Chicken and Cherry Tomatoes .................................. 42
Aromatic Chicken Cacciatore .......... 43
Garlic-Citrus Chicken with Potatoes ... 43

## 44 | Chapter 4 Pork, Beef, and Lamb

Classic Beef Bones Broth ............... 44
Beef Bolognese ........................... 44
Beef Meatballs with Tomatoes ......... 45
Pork and Pumpkin Stew ................. 45
Moroccan-style Lamb Shanks .......... 46
Gingered Pork Chops with Carrots ...... 46
Beef Roast with Vegetables ............. 47
Beef Pot Roast ............................ 47
Delicious Beef Stroganoff ............... 48
Beef with Bean Burrito Casserole ...... 48
Herbed Pork Loin with Dried Fruit and Leeks ..................................... 49

Stuffed Peppers with Ground Beef and Rice ............................................ 49
Beef Chili and Pinto Beans ............ 50
Pork Loin Roast with Potatoes ......... 50
Pulled Pork with Juicy Pineapple ...... 51
Pork and Celery with Mulled Cider ... 51
Tropical Thai-Style Curry Pork Tenderloin ................................. 52
Coffee Pork Tacos ........................ 52
Tangy Teriyaki Beef ..................... 53
Healthy Salsa Verde Pork ............... 53
Sweet Pork Tenderloin with Pomegranate Seeds ........................................ 54

## 55 | Chapter 5 Fish and Seafood

Trout with Carrot Mélange ............. 55
Shrimp and Scallop Tacos ............... 55
Cheesy Salmon with Root Vegetables 56
Cheesy Cod with White Potatoes ...... 56
Fish and Vegetable Risotto .............. 57
Lemony Salmon with Zucchini and Carrot 57
Spicy Monkfish with Sweet Potatoes ... 58
Shrimp with Corn Chowder ............ 58
Pesto Cod with White Bean Ratatouille 59
Shrimp with Cheesy Grits ............... 59
Cheesy Flounder with Almonds ........ 60

## 61 | Chapter 6 Soup, Chili and Stew

Herbed Split Pea and Carrot Soup ...... 61
Tangy Sweet Potato and Leek Soup ... 61
Creamy Wild Rice Stew with Mushrooms 62
Healthy Butternut Squash Soup ......... 62
Delicious BBQ Sauce .................... 63
Protein Soup ............................. 63
Peppercorn Chicken Stock .............. 64
Herbed Chicken Barley Stew ........... 64
Garlicky Fish Stock...................... 65
Wild Rice with Vegetable Soup ........ 65
Chickpea and Carrots Soup.............. 66
Delicious Bone Broth .................... 66
Creamy Zucchini Soup .................. 67
Beef & Butternut Squash Stew ......... 67
Turkey & Spinach Soup ................. 68
Spicy Chicken Tortilla Soup ............ 68
Creamy Cauliflower Soup ............... 69
Lemon Chickpea Soup .................. 69
Italian Chicken with Spaghetti Soup ... 70

## 71 | Chapter 7 Sauce, Dip and Dressings

Buffalo Cashews Dip .................... 71
Avocado Sauce ........................... 71

Classical Marinara Sauce ............... 72

Saucy Bolognese Sauce ................. 72

Tomato Sauce ............................ 73

Cheesy Artichoke and Spinach Sauce   73

Cheesy Buffalo Chicken Dip ........... 74

Spiced Smoky Barbecue Sauce ........ 74

Tangy Cinnamon-Berry Sauce ........ 75

Herbed Meat Sauce ..................... 75

Easy Rustic Marinara Sauce ........... 76

Italian-style Bolognese Sauce ........... 76

Creamy Cashews Sauce ................. 77

## 78 | Chapter 8 Desserts and Drinks

Blueberry-Peach Oats Cobbler ........ 78

Baked Apples with Pecans ............. 78

Coconut-Cacao Brownies .............. 79

Chai Latte ............................... 79

Chocolate Chip Lava Cake ............. 80

Stewed Fruit with Herbs ............... 80

Tangy Apple Cider Wassail.............. 81

Nutty Apple-Peach Crumble ........... 81

Healthy Berry Oats Crumble .......... 82

Peachy Brown Betty with Cranberries   82

Chocolate-Toffee Lava Cake ........... 83

Chocolate Nut Clusters ................. 83

Bananas Foster ......................... 84

Carrot Walnut Cake..................... 84

Orange Apple Cider .................... 85

Pumpkin Cheesecake ................... 85

Delicious Peach Mango Crisp........... 86

Bread Pudding with Dried Fruits ...... 86

## 87 | Conclusion

## 88 | Appendix 1 Measurement Conversion Chart

## 89 | Appendix 2 Recipes Index

# Introduction

A slow cooker is an electric device that cooks food for a long time at a low temperature. Slow cookers are excellent for breaking down and tenderizing big chunks of meat like pot roasts or beef stews because of this low-and-slow technique. But they have other options as well. A home cook's preferred method for making soups, ribs, dips, beverages, and bread is the slow cooker. In addition to its adaptability, a slow cooker has a lot of additional advantages, such as the ability to uniformly prepare food without needing to use your hands. Home chefs may now conduct other household chores, run errands, or start their day in the office because of this. Additionally, slow cookers are simple to use and typically only need to be plugged in. A slow cooker is simple to use. Simply turn on your slow cooker, add the ingredients for your selected meal, adjust the heat to low or high, depending on the recipe's directions, cover it, and let it simmer. If you don't want to consume your meal right away, you may either keep it warm in the slow cooker or turn the slow cooker off to turn off the heating element. I'm done now! For some dishes, such as ground beef chili or pork chops, it is necessary to brown some of the ingredients in a pan before adding them to the slow cooker. You might want to think about preheating your slow cooker in these circumstances.

# Fundamentals of Ninja Foodi 2-Basket Air Fryer

## What is Slow cooker?

A slow cooker is a type of cooking vessel that is frequently constructed of porcelain, metal, or ceramic. Typically, a heating element-containing electrical unit completely encircles it. The pot's bottom or all of its sides may have a heating element. A typical version is a straightforward metal heating plate with no edges at all, on which your cooking pot rests. All of them feature a glass, metal, or ceramic cover. These covers are intended to provide a low-pressure seal that keeps moisture within the pot. Food within the pot is cooked as a result of heat rising the pot's sides from the electric base. While cooking, slow cookers maintain a low, stable temperature. If your hectic schedule prohibits you from being in the kitchen before mealtime, a slow cooker is an answer. Dinner may be prepared in a slow cooker and left to cook while you are away from home. The typical slow cooker tends to consume less energy than an oven, even if it must be left on for several hours.

## How to Use Your Slow Cooker

**Slow Cook Low and High:**

1. Put the cooking pot into the main housing of the appliance. To turn the device on, plug it in and hit the power button.
2. Fill the cooking pot with the ingredients. Put a cover on the saucepan.
3. For LOW or HIGH, use the SLOW COOK button. The button's default setting is HIGH. The button will change

to WARM if you press it once more. It may be changed to LOW by pressing it a third time. It will cycle back to HIGH if you press it a fourth time. To set the time, press the TIME button once. To change the time, use the Up button, and to reduce it, press the Down button. The time may be changed in 15-minute intervals from 12 hours to 30 minutes.

4. The cooking cycle will begin 3 seconds after the cooking time has been selected.

5. While the food is cooking, the timing can be changed. When selecting your initial settings, press the TIME button and then utilize the Up and Down arrows.

6. The device will beep three times and then switch to Stay Warm for up to 12 hours when the countdown timer hits zero. As an alternative, you can push the Power button to halt cooking before the allotted time has passed (the unit will NOT switch to Stay Warm in this case).

7. Press the Power button to turn the device off when you are ready to do so. The Temp/Time display will show the word OFF.

### Warm function:

1. Put the cooking pot into the main housing of the appliance. To turn the device on, plug it in and hit the Power button.

2. Place the hot, cooked food in the pot and secure the lid. NOTE: Do not overfill the pot beyond two-thirds.

3. Select SLOW COOK from the menu. The default setting is HIGH. To pick WARM, press the button once more.

4. The warming cycle will begin 3 seconds after you pick WARM.

5. While the food is cooking, the timing can be changed. When selecting your initial settings, press the TEMP/TIME button and then utilize the Up and Down arrows.

6. Press the Power button to turn the device off when you are ready to do so. The word OFF will appear on the temperature/time display.

## Benefits of Using Slow Cooker

Unattended meal preparation. The main benefit of using a slow cooker is for safe, simple unattended cooking.

Keeping food warm at parties and events.

Saving money: A stove or oven consumes far more energy (kWh) than a slow cooker. A slow cooker won't heat your house as well as larger equipment will if you live somewhere with hot summers.

Of course, dining at home is less expensive. Low-and-slow cooking is ideal for inexpensive meals like slow cooker beans or difficult meat cuts like beef chuck roast and hog shoulder. However, these inexpensive items are simple to prepare on a stovetop or in an oven.

In addition to cooking in a wet environment for a prolonged length of time, slow cookers attain a simmer temperature of 209°F, which safely eliminates common pathogens including E. coli, salmonella, and botulism.

## What Can You Cook in a Slow Cooker?

A slow cooker can be used to prepare almost anything. You're probably most familiar with the hearty slow-cooked soups, stews, and main meals that benefit from boiling for hours on ends, such as chili, meatloaf, pulled pork sandwiches, and shredded chicken tacos. Dinnertime is also made simple with one-pot meals like casseroles cooked in a slow cooker.

Popular slow-cooker side dishes include baked potatoes and vegetable dishes since they take place in your oven for the main course. Additionally, attempt to cook softer veggies like peas, spinach, or zucchini later in the process. There are a few surprising uses for your slow cooker that you might not be aware of. Hashbrowns, oatmeal, and even cinnamon buns may be prepared in the slow cooker for hands-free breakfast and brunch meals. A party can also be prepared in advance with the help of slow-cooker appetizers like fondue or cheese dip. Try a slow-cooker spaghetti dish instead, but watch out for gritty pasta by not letting it simmer for too long.

Also, savory dishes don't have to be cooked in slow cookers. Cakes, puddings, candy clusters, and other sweet treats may be made with these slow-cooker dessert recipes. You can even treat yourself to a sweet slow cooker beverage, like hot chocolate or tropical-infused tea.

## Instructions for cooking:

### Pasta and rice

• If you're converting a recipe that calls for raw pasta, macaroni, or noodles, cook them on the stovetop for a brief period until they're just barely soft before putting them in the slow cooker.

• When substituting raw rice for cooked rice in a recipe that asks for cooked rice, add ¼ cup more liquid for every ¼ cup of raw rice. For the best outcomes, while cooking continuously all day, use long-grain converted rice.

### Beans

• Beans must be properly softened before being combined with sweet or acidic meals. Beans will not soften because of the hardening action of acid and sugar.

• Red kidney beans, in particular, should be cooked before being added to a dish. Bring to a boil three times as much unsalted water as the beans in a separate pot. Boil for 10 minutes, then lower the heat, cover the pot, and simmer the beans for 1 ½ hours, or until they are soft. If desired, soaking in water should be finished before boiling. After boiling or soaking, discard the water.

• Beans that have already been fully cooked can be used in place of dry beans.

### Vegetables

• Low cooking temperatures and slow cooking periods enable many vegetables, especially those with roots, to fully develop their flavors. In contrast to cooking them in the oven or on the stovetop, they don't frequently overcook in a slow cooker.

• Put the veggies in the slow cooker before the meat when making recipes that call for both roots vegetables and meat. In a slow cooker, rooted vegetables often cook more slowly than meat.

### Herbs and spices

• Hearty, fresh herbs like rosemary and thyme hold up well for meals with shorter cook times. Fresh herbs enhance flavor and color when added toward the end of the cooking cycle. Many fresh herbs' tastes will fade over extended cooking durations if used at the beginning. Use sparingly, taste toward the conclusion of the cooking cycle, and add the proper seasonings, including salt and pepper, if necessary. Ground and/or dried herbs and spices work well in slow cooking and may be added at the beginning. It is usually advised to taste the food and make any necessary seasoning adjustments right before serving because the flavor intensity of all herbs and spices can vary substantially based on their strength and shelf life.

## Liquids

- Always make sure the recipe calls for a proper amount of liquid to achieve the best results and avoid food from drying out or burning.
- Always fill the slow cooker to a minimum of ½ full and a maximum of ¾ full, and follow suggested cook times.

## Milk

- Milk, cream, and sour cream break down during extended cooking. Add in the final 15 to 30 minutes of cooking, if at all feasible. Milk can be substituted for condensed soups, which can also cook for a long period.

## Soups

- Two to three quarts of water are needed in certain soup recipes. Then, only enough water to cover the other soup ingredients in the slow cooker. When serving, add extra liquid if you like a thinner soup.
- Add 1 or 2 cups of water to milk-based soup recipes that call for no additional liquid during the first cooking process. When the cooking cycle is complete, gently whisk in the milk, cream, or sour cream because they will curdle if heated past the boiling point.

## Meats

- Trim the fat from meats, thoroughly clean or rinse, and then pat them dry with paper towels. While adding more flavor depth to the meal, browning the meat in a separate skillet or broiler enables fat to be drained off before slow simmering.

• Adjust the number of veggies or potatoes if you choose a smaller roast so that the slow cooker is ⅓ to ½ full.

• Always keep in mind that the specified cook time and meat size are only approximations. The unique cut, meat arrangement, and bone structure of a roast will determine the precise weight that can be cooked in a slow cooker.

• When preparing meat with pre-cooked beans, fruit, or lighter veggies like mushrooms, chopped onion, eggplant, or finely minced vegetables, cut the meat into smaller pieces. Food will be able to cook at the same rate thanks to this.

• Meats with less fat and connective tissue, such as beef chuck or pig shoulder, will cook more quickly than lean meats like chicken or pork tenderloin.

• The meat needs to be placed such that it lies inside the slow cooker and is not in contact with the lid.

• Cooking frozen meats (such as roasts or birds) requires adding at least 1 cup of heated liquid first. As a "cushion," the liquid will stop abrupt temperature swings. Meats should be cooked an extra 4 hours on LOW or 2 hours on HIGH in the majority of recipes that call for cubed frozen meat. Large frozen beef slices may require significantly more time to thaw and tenderize.

## Fish

• Because fish cooks fast, it should be added after the cooking process, between the final fifteen and one hours.

SPECIALTY Foods • To cook quickly and presentably, specialty dishes like stuffed chops or steak rolls, filled cabbage leaves, stuffed peppers, or baked apples can be stacked in a single layer.

Cleaning and Caring for Slow Cooker
Let the device cool after unplugging it from the wall socket.

NEVER let any liquid, including water, touch the main

housing.

Wipe a moist towel over the main housing and the control panel to clean them.

Warm, soapy water should be used to wash the cooking pot, steaming/roasting rack, and glass cover. Dishwasher cleaning is possible for the cooking pot, steaming/roasting rack, and glass lid.

Every time you use a part, dry it.

Fill the cooking pot with water and let it soak before cleaning if food residue has trapped on it. AVOID using scouring pads. Use a non-abrasive cleaner or liquid detergent with a nylon pad or brush if scouring is required.

## Cooking Tips and Warnings

Always fill the slow cooker ½ to ¾ full to adhere to stated cook times to prevent over- or under-cooking.

Sparingly fill the slow cooker. Never fill it more than ¾ full to avoid spills.

Always cook for the prescribed amount of time with the lid on.

During the first two hours of cooking, do not remove the lid.

Wear oven gloves whenever you handle the lid or any pot.

After cooking and before cleaning, unplug all electronics.

To avoid overcooking and overflow, always fill your slow cooker to about three-quarters of the way.

Never peek! Heat is released when the lid is opened to check on your meal, which increases cooking time.

Yes, practically any recipe can be converted into a slow cooker dinner. Use these instructions or locate a similar recipe that has been written as a slow cooker recipe.

The finest companion for a meal planner is a slow cooker. One-pot slow cooker recipes make sure you're not left with a lot of dirty dishes, and freezer-friendly slow cooker dinners ensure you can always have supper on hand.

When used, this gadget produces heat. Avoid touching warm surfaces. Use knobs or handles.

Avoid submerging cords, plugs, or appliances in water or other liquids to prevent electric shock.

Children or those with impaired physical, sensory, or mental skills should not use this equipment.

Any appliance used near youngsters must be closely supervised. The device shouldn't be used by kids as playthings.

When not in use, before putting on or taking off parts, and before cleaning, unplug from the outlet. Before putting components on or taking them off, as well as before cleaning, let them cool. Turn off any controls before unplugging the power wire from the socket to detach it. Never cut the power by tugging on the cable.

Never use an appliance that has a broken cable or plug, isn't working properly, or has otherwise sustained harm. Never try to repair or splice a broken cord. Send the appliance back to the maker for inspection, maintenance, or adjusting.

Injury may result from using accessory attachments that the appliance manufacturer does not suggest.

Use only indoors; never outside or for profit.

Do not allow the cord to touch hot surfaces or dangle over the edge of a table or counter.

Placement on or near moist surfaces, near heat sources like hot gas or electric burners, or inside a heated oven is not recommended.

When transferring an appliance that contains hot oil or other hot liquids, extreme caution must be utilized.

Before handling the slow cooker, let it cool.

When opening the lid during or following a cooking cycle, exercise care. Burns can occur when steam escapes.

Use the equipment just for what it was designed for. Injuries may result from misuse.

Only for use on domestic countertops. Keep your distance

from the wall and all sides at least 6 inches (152 mm). Always operate the equipment on a flat, dry surface.

A hot pot should not be filled with chilled food or cold drinks to prevent rapid temperature fluctuations.

Always look for cracks, chips, or other damage on the lid. If the cover is broken, don't use it since it can break while you're using it.

## Frequently Asked Questions

### 1. What is the difference between my LOW and HIGH settings?

It only depends on how long it takes to get to the simmer point because HIGH and LOW are stable at the same temperature. The amount of time needed to cook food to the point where taste and texture are at their best depends on the cut and weight of the meat after it reaches the simmering phase. (You can cook most meals on either HIGH or LOW.

### 2. How full should my slow cooker be?

For optimal results, a slow cooker should be at least half filled.

### 3. Does water in a slow cooker evaporate?

Evaporation occurs relatively seldom in slow cookers. Remember that your finished result may be thicker when converting a recipe intended for the stovetop; additional water added throughout or after cooking will help thin it down.

### 4. Do I need to stir while my slow cooker cooks?

You don't need to stir during cooking for the majority of recipes. When you open the lid to stir, the heat within your slow cooker diminishes, lengthening the cooking time.

### 5. Is it okay to let my slow cooker simmer while I'm away from home?

You can, indeed. Place your slow cooker on a spotless, level surface to make sure it is secure when cooking unattended. To prevent the cable from angling off the counter, make sure nothing is touching your crock-pot and tuck it up and out of the way. It could be a good idea to prevent your pets from entering the kitchen if you have curious animals that might be enticed to check what is cooking while you are away.

### 6. How can I avoid over- or undercooking food?

Except for some cakes and custards, always fill the slow cooker halfway to three-quarters of the way full to adhere to suggested cook times. Additionally, if a recipe specifies a range of cooking times, cook for the shortest time possible, check your meal, and then cook longer if necessary.

### 7. How can I prevent my food in the slow cooker from becoming mushy?

To prevent your food from becoming excessively wet in your slow cooker, here are a few tips and tactics. One of the easiest methods is to routinely check on what's cooking, either with a glance or a more precise temperature reading.

### 8. What is the duration of the Keep Warm setting?

4 hours (standard)

### 9. Are BPA-free slow cooker liners available?

By US FDA 21CFR, 177.1500 - Nylon resins for cooking temperatures up to 400°F - the Slow Cooker Liners are BPA-free.

# 4-Week Diet Plan

## Week 1

**Day 1:**
Breakfast: Sweet Potato & Onion Casserole
Lunch: Vegetable Broth
Dinner: Spicy Whole Chicken
Dessert: Blueberry-Peach Oats Cobbler

**Day 2:**
Breakfast: Hard-Boiled Eggs
Lunch: Veggie and Quinoa Casserole
Dinner: Beef Bolognese
Dessert: Baked Apples with Pecans

**Day 3:**
Breakfast: Chicken-Apple Sausage
Lunch: Easy Spaghetti Squash
Dinner: Pork and Pumpkin Stew
Dessert: Coconut-Cacao Brownies

**Day 4:**
Breakfast: Beet & Spinach Frittata
Lunch: Beans Stuffed Sweet Potatoes
Dinner: Shrimp and Scallop Tacos
Dessert: Chai Latte

**Day 5:**
Breakfast: Cinnamon Apple Pie Oats
Lunch: Vegan Navy Beans with Cranberries
Dinner: Chicken Veggie Broth
Dessert: Chocolate Chip Lava Cake

**Day 6:**
Breakfast: Cheese Veggie Frittata
Lunch: Healthy Beans
Dinner: Beef Meatballs with Tomatoes
Dessert: Carrot Walnut Cake

**Day 7:**
Breakfast: Mixed Berries Butter Toast
Lunch: Cheesy Spring Vegetable Pasta
Dinner: Moroccan-style Lamb Shanks
Dessert: Stewed Fruit with Herbs

## Week 2

**Day 1:**
Breakfast: Cheesy Oatmeal with Spinach
Lunch: Garlic, Spinach and Beans Chili
Dinner: Cheesy Cod with White Potatoes
Dessert: Nutty Apple-Peach Crumble

**Day 2:**
Breakfast: Herbed Root Vegetable Hash
Lunch: Mashed Root Vegetables
Dinner: Healthy Salsa Chicken
Dessert: Peachy Brown Betty with Cranberries

**Day 3:**
Breakfast: Spicy Eggs in Purgatory
Lunch: Udon Noodle Soup with Veggie
Dinner: Beef Roast with Vegetables
Dessert: Healthy Berry Oats Crumble

**Day 4:**
Breakfast: Multi-Grain Granola with Cherries
Lunch: Collard Greens with Bacon
Dinner: Coffee Pork Tacos
Dessert: Chocolate-Toffee Lava Cake

**Day 5:**
Breakfast: Cheesy Omelet Casserole
Lunch: Onion & Bell Pepper Stuffed Tomatoes
Dinner: Fish and Vegetable Risotto
Dessert: Pumpkin Cheesecake

**Day 6:**
Breakfast: Hot Coconut Cereal
Lunch: Cheesy Potato Gratin
Dinner: Thai Chicken Curry
Dessert: Chocolate Nut Clusters

**Day 7:**
Breakfast: Apple and Granola Casserole
Lunch: Roasted Vegetables
Dinner: Healthy Salsa Verde Pork
Dessert: Bananas Foster

## Week 3

**Day 1:**
Breakfast: Dates Millet Porridge
Lunch: Roasted butternut Squash Purée
Dinner: Beef with Bean Burrito Casserole
Dessert: Carrot Walnut Cake

**Day 2:**
Breakfast: Cranberries Quinoa-Oat Cereal
Lunch: Sweet & Sour Beets with Onions
Dinner: Shrimp with Cheesy Grits
Dessert: Delicious Peach Mango Crisp

**Day 3:**
Breakfast: Creamy Pumpkin Steel-Cut Oats
Lunch: Herbed Greens with Onions
Dinner: Chicken Chili with Beans
Dessert: Bread Pudding with Dried Fruits

**Day 4:**
Breakfast: Tropical Farro with Mango and Nuts
Lunch: Delicious Turkey Stuffed Peppers
Dinner: Beef Chili and Pinto Beans
Dessert: Blueberry-Peach Oats Cobbler

**Day 5:**
Breakfast: Nutty Granola with Dried Berries
Lunch: Garlicky Mashed Red Potatoes
Dinner: Stuffed Peppers with Ground Beef and Rice
Dessert: Baked Apples with Pecans

**Day 6:**
Breakfast: Healthy Vegetable Frittata
Lunch: Bacon Cabbage Casserole
Dinner: Pulled Pork with Juicy Pineapple
Dessert: Coconut-Cacao Brownies

**Day 7:**
Breakfast: Spinach Ham Quiche
Lunch: Veggie and Quinoa Casserole
Dinner: Shrimp with Corn Chowder
Dessert: Chai Latte

## Week 4

**Day 1:**
Breakfast: Hard-Boiled Eggs
Lunch: Easy Spaghetti Squash
Dinner: Cheesy Salsa Chicken
Dessert: Chocolate Chip Lava Cake

**Day 2:**
Breakfast: Chicken-Apple Sausage
Lunch: Beans Stuffed Sweet Potatoes
Dinner: Tropical Thai-Style Curry Pork Tenderloin
Dessert: Stewed Fruit with Herbs

**Day 3:**
Breakfast: Beet & Spinach Frittata
Lunch: Vegetable Broth
Dinner: Garlicky Turkey Breasts
Dessert: Nutty Apple-Peach Crumble

**Day 4:**
Breakfast: Cinnamon Apple Pie Oats
Lunch: Vegan Navy Beans with Cranberries
Dinner: Pork Loin Roast with Potatoes
Dessert: Peachy Brown Betty with Cranberries

**Day 5:**
Breakfast: Cheese Veggie Frittata
Lunch: Healthy Beans
Dinner: Beef Pot Roast
Dessert: Chocolate-Toffee Lava Cake

**Day 6:**
Breakfast: Mixed Berries Butter Toast
Lunch: Cheesy Spring Vegetable Pasta
Dinner: Lemony Salmon with Zucchini and Carrot
Dessert: Pumpkin Cheesecake

**Day 7:**
Breakfast: Cheesy Oatmeal with Spinach
Lunch: Mashed Root Vegetables
Dinner: Southwest Chicken with Zucchini
Dessert: Chocolate Nut Clusters

# Chapter 1 Breakfast

## Sweet Potato & Onion Casserole

Prep time: 15 minutes | Cook time: 6-8 hours | Serves: 6

3 tablespoons extra-virgin olive oil, plus more for coating the slow cooker
2 pounds sweet potatoes, diced
1 red bell pepper, seeded and diced
½ medium onion, finely diced
1 teaspoon garlic powder
1 teaspoon sea salt
1 teaspoon dried rosemary, minced
½ teaspoon freshly ground black pepper

1. Grease the slow cooker with olive oil. 2. Put the sweet potatoes along with the red bell pepper and onion in the slow cooker. Drizzle the olive oil over the vegetables. 3. Scatter in the garlic powder, salt, rosemary, and pepper. Toss to coat the sweet potatoes with seasonings. 4. Cover the slow cooker and set it to low temp setting. Cook for 6 to 8 hours and serve.
**Per Serving:** Calories 296; Fat 11g; Sodium 705mg; Carbs 48g; Fiber 7g; Sugar 10g; Protein 4g

## Hard-Boiled Eggs

Prep time: 15 minutes | Cook time: 2½ hours | Serves: 6

6 large eggs
1 tablespoon distilled white vinegar

1. Place the eggs in bottom of the slow cooker. 2. Add enough water to just cover the eggs. Add the vinegar. 3. Cover the slow cooker and set to high temp setting. Cook for 2½ hours. 4. Let cool before serving.
**Per Serving:** Calories 74; Fat 5g; Sodium 70mg; Carbs 1g; Fiber 0g; Sugar 1g; Protein 6g

## Chicken-Apple Sausage

**Prep time: 15 minutes | Cook time: 6-8 hours | Serves: 6**

- 1-pound ground chicken
- ½ medium apple, peeled and minced
- 1 teaspoon sea salt
- ½ teaspoon freshly ground black pepper
- ½ teaspoon dried parsley flakes
- ½ teaspoon garlic powder
- ½ teaspoon dried basil leaves
- ¼ teaspoon ground cinnamon

1. In a bowl, combine the chicken, apple, salt, pepper, parsley flakes, garlic powder, basil, and cinnamon. Mix well. Spread the chicken mix into slow cooker in thin layer. 2. Cover the slow cooker and set to low temp setting. Cook for 6 to 8 hours, or until the meat is completely cooked through. 3. Loosen the chicken from around the edges with help of spatula and transfer to a cutting board. Cut into desired shapes and serve.

**Per Serving:** Calories 210; Fat 12g; Sodium 672mg; Carbs 4g; Fiber 1g; Sugar 2g; Protein 21g

---

## Beet & Spinach Frittata

**Prep time: 15 minutes | Cook time: 5-7 hours | Serves: 6**

- 1 tablespoon extra-virgin olive oil
- 8 large eggs
- 1 cup packed fresh spinach leaves, chopped
- 1 cup diced peeled golden beets
- ½ medium onion, diced
- ¼ cup unsweetened almond milk
- ¾ teaspoon sea salt
- ½ teaspoon garlic powder
- ½ teaspoon dried basil leaves
- Freshly ground black pepper

1. Grease the slow cooker with the olive oil. 2. In a bowl, combine the eggs, spinach, beets, onion, almond milk, salt, garlic powder, and basil, and spice with pepper. 3. Mix all until well incorporated and pour the custard into the slow cooker. 4. Cover the slow cooker and set to low temp setting. Cook for 5 to 7 hours until the eggs are completely set, and serve.

**Per Serving:** Calories 202; Fat 14g; Sodium 606mg; Carbs 6g; Fiber 1g; Sugar 4g; Protein 13g

## Cinnamon Apple Pie Oats

Prep time: 15 minutes | Cook time: 6-8 hours | Serves: 4

1 to 2 tablespoons butter or coconut oil
4 cups unsweetened flax milk or coconut milk
1 cup rolled oats
1 to 2 cups chopped peeled apples or pears
2 tablespoons pure maple syrup
1 to 2 teaspoons ground cinnamon
1 teaspoon vanilla extract
½ cup nut butter, for topping

1. Grease the bottom and sides of a slow cooker with the butter. 2. Add the milk, oats, apples, maple syrup, cinnamon, and vanilla in pot. Mix well. 3. Cover and cook on low temp for 6 to 8 hours, until the oats and apples are soft and the oatmeal has thickened to desire consistency. 4. Serve the oats in a bowl topped with nut butter.
**Per Serving:** Calories 205; Fat 9g; Sodium 47mg; Carbs 28g; Fiber 4g; Sugar 9g; Protein 4g

---

## Cheese Veggie Frittata

Prep time: 10 minutes | Cook time: 6-8 hours | Serves: 6-8

1 tablespoon extra-virgin olive oil
12 large eggs
¾ cup 2 percent milk
1 teaspoon sea salt
2 teaspoons Dijon mustard
¼ teaspoon ground black pepper
1 tablespoon onion powder
1 pound frozen hash browns
2 cups chopped or diced cored red, yellow, or orange bell peppers
1 (9.6-ounce) package cooked sausage, chopped into bite-size pieces
1½ cups shredded Cheddar cheese, divided
2 cups baby spinach

1. Grease a slow cooker with the olive oil. 2. In a bowl, Mix well the eggs, milk, salt, mustard, black pepper, and onion powder. 3. Put the hash browns in the slow cooker, the bell peppers, sausage, cheese, the spinach, and the egg mixture. Do not stir. Cover the slow cooker and cook on low temp for 6 to 8 hours, until the eggs have set. 4. Remove the lid and add the remaining cheese. 5. Cover the pot with the lid again and let sit for about 5 minutes, until the cheese has melted. Serve warm.
**Per Serving:** Calories 484; Fat 31g; Sodium 868mg; Carbs 21g; Fiber 3g; Sugar 4g; Protein 30g

## Mixed Berries Butter Toast

Prep time: 15 minutes | Cook time: 4 hours | Serves: 6

Nonstick cooking spray, for coating the slow cooker
1 cup coconut sugar
4 tablespoons (½ stick) butter, melted
1¼ teaspoons ground cinnamon
12 whole-grain bread slices
1½ cups mixed fresh blueberries and raspberries, plus more for serving
6 large eggs
1½ cups 2 percent milk
1 tablespoon vanilla extract
½ teaspoon sea salt
¾ cup almond butter, for topping
¾ cup light whipped cream, for topping

1. Grease a slow cooker with cooking spray. 2. In a bowl, mix the sugar, butter, and cinnamon. 3. Spread one-third of the cinnamon-sugar butter on the slow cooker pot. 4. Arrange 6 bread slices on top of the cinnamon-sugar butter. 5. Cover the bread with another third of the cinnamon-sugar butter, then sprinkle the berries over the top. 6. Layer the 6 bread slices on top of the berries, and cover with the third of the cinnamon-sugar butter. 7. In a bowl, mix the eggs, milk, vanilla, and salt. 8. Pour the egg mixture over the bread layers. Do not stir. Cover the slow cooker, cook on low temp setting for 4 hours, until the French toast is golden brown and set on top. 9. Serve the French toast with more berries and top with almond butter and whipped cream, if desired.

**Per Serving:** Calories 593; Fat 18g; Sodium 640mg; Carbs 85g; Fiber 10g; Sugar 45g; Protein 22g

## Cheesy Oatmeal with Spinach

Prep time: 10 minutes | Cook time: 7-8 hours | Serves: 8

3 cups steel-cut oatmeal
2 shallots, peeled and minced
5 cups Roasted Vegetable Broth
1 cup water
1 teaspoon dried basil leaves
½ teaspoon dried thyme leaves
¼ teaspoon salt
¼ teaspoon freshly ground black pepper
½ cup grated Parmesan cheese
2 cups chopped baby spinach leaves
2 tablespoons chopped fresh basil

1. In a slow cooker pot, add the oatmeal, shallots, vegetable broth, water, basil, thyme, salt, and pepper and stir. Cover the slow cooker and cook on low temp for 7 to 8 hours, or until the oatmeal is tender. 2. Stir in the Parmesan cheese, spinach, and basil, and let stand, covered, for another 5 minutes. Stir and serve.

**Per Serving:** Calories 262; Fat 5g; Sodium 172mg; Carbs 43g; Fiber 6g; Sugar 2g; Protein 8g

## Herbed Root Vegetable Hash

**Prep time: 20 minutes | Cook time: 7-8 hours | Serves: 8**

- 4 Yukon Gold potatoes, chopped
- 2 russet potatoes, chopped
- 1 large parsnip, peeled and chopped
- 3 large carrots, peeled and chopped
- 2 onions, chopped
- 2 garlic cloves, minced
- 2 tablespoons olive oil
- ¼ cup Roasted Vegetable Broth
- ½ teaspoon salt
- 1 teaspoon dried thyme leaves

1. In a slow cooker, mix all of the ingredients and vegetables. Cover the slow cooker, cook on low temp setting for 7 to 8 hours. 2. Stir the hash well and serve.

**Per Serving:** Calories 150; Fat 4g; Sodium 176mg; Carbs 28g; Fiber 4g; Sugar 4g; Protein 3g

## Spicy Eggs in Purgatory

**Prep time: 15 minutes | Cook time: 7-8 hours | Serves: 8**

- 2½ pounds Roma tomatoes, chopped
- 2 onions, chopped
- 2 garlic cloves, chopped
- 1 teaspoon paprika
- ½ teaspoon ground cumin
- ½ teaspoon dried marjoram leaves
- 1 cup Roasted Vegetable Broth
- 8 large eggs
- 2 red chili peppers, minced
- ½ cup chopped flat-leaf parsley

1. In a slow cooker, mix the tomatoes, onions, garlic, paprika, cumin, marjoram, and vegetable broth, and stir to mix. Cover the slow cooker, cook on low temp for 7 to 8 hours, or until a sauce has formed. 2. Break the eggs one by one into the sauce; do not stir. 3. Cover and cook on high temp setting temp setting until the egg whites are completely set and the yolk is thickened, about 20 minutes. Sprinkle the eggs with the minced red chili peppers. 4. Sprinkle with the parsley for vibrant color and serve.

**Per Serving:** Calories 116; Fat 5g; Sodium 102mg; Carbs 10g; Fiber 2g; Sugar 5g; Protein 8g

## Multi-Grain Granola with Cherries

**Prep time: 15 minutes | Cook time: 3½ hours | Serves: 40**

5 cups regular oatmeal
4 cups barley flakes
3 cups buckwheat flakes
2 cups whole almonds
2 cups whole walnuts
½ cup honey
2 teaspoons ground cinnamon
1 tablespoon vanilla extract
2 cups golden raisins
2 cups dried cherries

1. In a slow cooker, mix the oatmeal, barley flakes, buckwheat flakes, almonds, and walnuts. 2. In a bowl, mix the honey, cinnamon, and vanilla, and mix well. Drizzle this mixture over the food in the slow cooker and stir to coat. 3. Partially cover the slow cooker. Cook on low temp setting for 3½ to 5 hours, stirring twice during cooking time, until the toasted. 4. Remove the granola from the slow cooker and spread on two large baking sheets. Add the raisins and cherries to the granola and stir gently. 5. Let the granola cool.
**Per Serving:** Calories 161; Fat 4g; Sodium 32mg; Carbs 32g; Fiber 3g; Sugar 28g; Protein 2g

## Cheesy Omelet Casserole

**Prep time: 10 minutes | Cook time: 10-12 hours | Serves: 4**

32 oz. frozen hash brown potatoes
1 lb. of bacon diced, crumbled
1 onion, diced
1 green bell pepper, diced
1½ cups Cheddar or Monterey Jack cheese, shredded
1 dozen eggs
1 cup milk
1 teaspoon salt
1 teaspoon pepper

1. In layers, place potatoes on a slow cooker, followed by bacon, onions, green pepper and cheese. 2. Make two or three more layers ending with cheese. Blend the eggs, milk, salt and pepper. Pour the mixture into the slow cooker, cover the lid and turn on low temp setting. 3. Cook for 10-12 hours.
**Per Serving:** Calories 208; Fat 4g; Sodium 329mg; Carbs 39g; Fiber 6g; Sugar 13g; Protein 7g

## Hot Coconut Cereal

**Prep time: 10 minutes | Cook time: 7-9 hours | Serves: 4**

¼ cup cracked wheat
¼ cup steel cut oats
¼ cup coconut, sweetened or unsweetened
3 cups water
¼ teaspoon salt, or to taste

¼ cup pearl barley
¼ cup brown rice
½ cup of light cream or half-and-half
¼ cup dried cranberries

1. Combine all ingredients except cream or half-and-half in a slow cooker. 2. Cover the slow cooker, cook on low temp for 7 to 9 hours. 3. Add ½ cup of light cream and cook for another 10 minutes. Garnish with cinnamon sugar or dried cranberries. 4. Serve with milk.
**Per Serving:** Calories 324; Fat 19g; Sodium 17mg; Carbs 17g; Fiber 1g; Sugar 3g; Protein 22g

## Apple and Granola Casserole

**Prep time: 15 minutes | Cook time: 5-7 hours | Serves: 4**

3 cups peeled, sliced tart apples
1 teaspoon cinnamon
2 cups granola cereal

¼ cup honey
3 tablespoon melted butter

1. Grease slow cooker with nonstick cooking spray. Put the apples into the slow cooker and sprinkle with the cinnamon and granola. 2. In a bowl, stir the honey and butter. Sprinkle over the apple mixture. Mix everything gently. 3. Cover the slow cooker and cook on low temp for 5 to 7 hours. Check for doneness with a fork. 4. Serve with fruit, yogurt or ice cream, if desired.
**Per Serving:** Calories 274; Fat 19g; Sodium 333mg; Carbs 5g; Fiber 1g; Sugar 4g; Protein 16g

## Dates Millet Porridge

**Prep time: 10 minutes | Cook time: 8 hours | Serves: 8**

1¼ cups millet
4 Medjool dates, pitted and finely chopped
3 cups unsweetened almond milk, divided
3 cups water
Pinch kosher salt

1 (4-inch) cinnamon stick or ½ teaspoon ground cinnamon
1 teaspoon ground cardamom
2 teaspoons pure vanilla extract
Berries, for serving
Slivered almonds, for serving

1. In a slow cooker, combine the millet, dates, 2½ cups of almond milk, the water, salt, cinnamon, cardamom, and vanilla. 2. Cover the slow cooker, cook on low temp for 8 hours, until the liquid is absorbed. 3. stir well. Pour in the ½ cup of almond milk. 4. Place in serving bowls and top with berries and almonds

**Per Serving:** Calories 43; Fat 1g; Sodium 9mg; Carbs 9g; Fiber 1g; Sugar 8g; Protein 0g

---

## Cranberries Quinoa-Oat Cereal

**Prep time: 5 minutes | Cook time: 2½ hours | Serves: 8**

¾ cup quinoa (any color), rinsed
1½ cups gluten-free rolled oats
½ cup unsweetened dried cranberries
Pinch kosher salt
½ teaspoon ground cardamom

4 cups unsweetened vanilla almond milk
1 (3-inch) cinnamon stick or 1 teaspoon ground cinnamon
Maple syrup, for serving
Shelled pumpkin seeds, for serving
Chopped walnuts, for serving

1. In a slow cooker, combine the quinoa, oats, cranberries, salt, and cardamom. Stir in the milk, then add the cinnamon stick. 2. Cover the slow cooker and cook on high temp for 2 to 2½ hours, until most of the liquid is absorbed. 3. Spoon into serving bowls and top with maple syrup, pumpkin seeds, and walnuts.

**Per Serving:** Calories 320; Fat 19g; Sodium 822mg; Carbs 12g; Fiber 1g; Sugar 3g; Protein 25g

## Creamy Pumpkin Steel-Cut Oats

**Prep time: 5 minutes | Cook time: 8 hours | Serves: 8**

1½ cups gluten-free steel-cut oats
6 cups water
¼ cup pumpkin purée
2 tablespoons maple syrup
1 tablespoon pumpkin pie spice

2 teaspoons pure vanilla extract
Pinch kosher salt
Chopped apples of choice, for serving
Chopped walnuts or pecans, for serving
Unsweetened dried cranberries, for serving

1. In a slow cooker, combine the oats, water, pumpkin purée, maple syrup, pie spice, vanilla, and salt. 2. Cover the slow cooker, cook on low temp for 7 to 8 hours, until the water is absorbed and the oats are creamy. 3. Stir well. Spoon into serving bowls and top with apples, nuts, and cranberries.
**Per Serving:** Calories 276; Fat 4g; Sodium 57mg; Carbs 57g; Fiber 4g; Sugar 35g; Protein 5g

## Tropical Farro with Mango and Nuts

**Prep time: 5 minutes | Cook time: 3 hours | Serves: 6**

1 cup farro, rinsed
1 (16.9-ounce) carton coconut water or 2 cups water
1 teaspoon pure vanilla extract

8 ounces frozen mango chunks, partially thawed
1 (4-inch) cinnamon stick or 1 teaspoon ground cinnamon
6 tablespoons chopped unsalted macadamia nuts

1. In a slow cooker, stir the farro, coconut water, and vanilla. Add the mango and cinnamon stick. 2. Cover the slow cooker and cook on high temp for 2½ to 3 hours, until the farro is chewy but tender. 3. Spoon the farro into serving bowls and top each with 1 tablespoon of macadamia nuts.
**Per Serving:** Calories 245; Fat 14g; Sodium 12mg; Carbs 12g; Fiber 2g; Sugar 4g; Protein 15g

## Nutty Granola with Dried Berries

**Prep time: 10 minutes | Cook time: 6 hours | Serves: 6**

Cooking spray
3 cups old-fashioned rolled oats
2 cups almonds, pecans, or walnuts
¼ cup unsweetened coconut flakes
½ cup dried cranberries, berries, or cherries
¼ cup chia seeds
1 teaspoon ground cinnamon
½ teaspoon salt
¼ teaspoon ground nutmeg
¼ cup coconut oil
½ cup honey or maple syrup
1 teaspoon vanilla extract

1. Grease slow cooker with cooking spray. Combine the oats, nuts, coconut flakes, dried fruit, chia seeds, cinnamon, salt, and nutmeg in the slow cooker. 2. In a bowl, melt the coconut oil in the microwave. Whisk in the honey and vanilla. Pour the oil mixture into the slow cooker, stirring. 3. Cover the slow cooker and cook on low temp for 6 hours. 4. Transfer the granola to a baking sheet to cool. Store in an airtight container

**Per Serving:** Calories 197; Fat 2g; Sodium 46mg; Carbs 46g; Fiber 4g; Sugar 26g; Protein 4g

---

## Healthy Vegetable Frittata

**Prep time: 10 minutes | Cook time: 8-9 hours | Serves: 12**

2 red or green bell peppers, seeded and diced
1 medium onion, diced
½ cup diced tomatoes
1 small zucchini, diced
8 ounces sweet potato, peeled and shredded
Handful fresh parsley leaves
12 large eggs
1 cup unsweetened almond milk
1 teaspoon salt
½ teaspoon freshly ground black pepper

1. Combine the bell peppers, onion, tomatoes, zucchini, sweet potato, and parsley in the slow cooker. 2. In a bowl, whisk the eggs, almond milk, salt, and pepper. Pour the egg mixture over of the vegetables in the slow cooker. 3. Cover the slow cooker and cook on low temp for 8 or 9 hours, or until the eggs are set.

**Per Serving:** Calories 232; Fat 12g; Sodium 578mg; Carbs 5g; Fiber 1g; Sugar 1g; Protein 7g

## Spinach Ham Quiche

**Prep time: 10 minutes | Cook time: 5 hours | Serves: 6**

Nonstick cooking spray
4 large eggs
1 cup half-and-half
1 cup shredded sharp Cheddar cheese
3 cups fresh baby spinach leaves
2 cups cubed ham
½ teaspoon salt
¼ teaspoon freshly ground black pepper

1. Grease the slow cooker with nonstick cooking spray. 2. In a bowl, beat the eggs. Add the half-and-half, Cheddar cheese, spinach, ham, salt, and pepper and stir to combine. Pour the mix into the slow cooker. 3. Cover the slow cooker and cook on low temp for 5 hours. 4. Let it sit for 15 minutes before serving.
**Per Serving:** Calories 291; Fat 20.6g; Sodium 369mg; Carbs 2.7g; Fiber 1.3g; Sugar 1.5g; Protein 23.9g

# Chapter 2 Vegetables and Sides

## Vegetable Broth

**Prep time: 15 minutes | Cook time: 6-8 hours | Serves: 12**

Extra-virgin olive oil, for greasing
6 cups veggie scraps (peels and pieces of carrots, celery, onions, garlic)
12 cups filtered water
½ medium onion, roughly chopped
2 garlic cloves, roughly chopped
1 parsley sprig
¾ teaspoon sea salt
½ teaspoon dried oregano
½ teaspoon dried basil leaves
2 bay leaves

1. Grease the slow cooker with olive oil. 2. In the slow cooker, combine the veggie scraps, water, onion, garlic, parsley, salt, oregano, basil, and bay leaves. 3. Cover the slow cooker and set to low temp setting. Cook for 6 to 8 hours. 4. Pour the broth through a fine-mesh sieve set over a bowl, discarding the veggie scraps.
**Per Serving:** Calories 160; Fat 11.8g; Sodium 255mg; Carbs 9.6g; Fiber 3.9g; Sugar 2g; Protein 7.6g

## Veggie and Quinoa Casserole

**Prep time: 15 minutes | Cook time: 4-6 hours | Serves: 6**

2 cups quinoa, rinsed well
4 cups vegetable broth
¼ cup sliced carrots
¼ cup corn kernels
¼ cup green peas
¼ cup diced scallion
1 tablespoon sesame oil
1 teaspoon garlic powder
1 teaspoon sea salt
Dash red pepper flakes

1. In slow cooker, combine the quinoa, broth, carrots, corn, peas, scallion, sesame oil, garlic powder, salt, and red pepper flakes. 2. Cover the slow cooker and set to low temp setting. Cook for 4 to 6 hours, fluff, and serve.
**Per Serving:** Calories 221; Fat 14g; Sodium 221mg; Carbs 6g; Fiber 4g; Sugar 1g; Protein 11g

## Easy Spaghetti Squash

**Prep time: 15 minutes | Cook time: 8 hours | Serves: 6**

1 spaghetti squash, washed well

2 cups water

1. Using a fork, poke 10 to 15 holes all around the outside of the spaghetti squash. Put the squash and the water in slow cooker. 2. Cover the slow cooker and set to low temp setting. Cook for 8 hours. 3. Transfer the squash to a cutting board. Let sit for 15 minutes to cool. 4. Halve the squash lengthwise. Using a spoon, scrape the seeds out of the center of the squash. 5. Then, using a fork, scrape at the flesh until it shreds into a spaghetti-like texture. Serve warm.
**Per Serving:** Calories 116; Fat 8.4g; Sodium 542mg; Carbs 0.9g; Fiber 0.2g; Sugar 0.1g; Protein 9.1g

## Beans Stuffed Sweet Potatoes

**Prep time: 15 minutes | Cook time: 6-7 hours | Serves: 4**

4 medium sweet potatoes
1 cup "Refried" Beans
4 tablespoons chopped scallions (both white and green parts)
1 avocado, peeled, pitted, and quartered

1. Wash the sweet potatoes, but do not dry them. Put the damp sweet potatoes in slow cooker. 2. Cover the slow cooker and set to low temp setting. Cook for 6 to 7 hours. A fork should easily poke through when they are done. 3. Carefully remove the hot sweet potatoes from the slow cooker. Slice each one lengthwise about halfway through. Mash the revealed flesh with a fork, and fill the opening with ¼ cup of beans. 4. Top each with scallions and a quarter of the avocado and serve.
**Per Serving:** Calories 200; Fat 5g; Sodium 269mg; Carbs 4g; Fiber 1g; Sugar 1g; Protein 5g

## Vegan Navy Beans with Cranberries

**Prep time: 15 minutes | Cook time: 7-8 hours | Serves: 6**

2 cups dried navy beans, soaked in water overnight, drained, and rinsed
6 cups vegetable broth
¼ cup dried cranberries
1 medium sweet onion, diced
½ cup all-natural ketchup
3 tablespoons extra-virgin olive oil
2 tablespoons maple syrup
2 tablespoons molasses
1 tablespoon apple cider vinegar
1 teaspoon Dijon mustard
1 teaspoon sea salt
½ teaspoon garlic powder

1. In slow cooker, combine the beans, broth, cranberries, onion, ketchup, olive oil, maple syrup, molasses, vinegar, mustard, salt, and garlic powder. 2. Cover the slow cooker and set to low temp setting. Cook for 7 to 8 hours and serve.
**Per Serving:** Calories 374; Fat 31.7g; Sodium 287mg; Carbs 7g; Fiber 3g; Sugar 1g; Protein 18.7g

## Healthy Beans

**Prep time: 8 hours | Cook time: 7-8 hours | Serves: 6**

1 pound dried beans, any kind
Water

1. Put the beans in a bowl or in slow cooker and cover with water. 2. Let soak for a minimum of 8 hours, or overnight, at room temperature. 3. Drain and rinse the beans well. Put them in slow cooker and cover with 2 inches of fresh water. 4. Cover the slow cooker and set to low temp setting. Cook for 7 to 8 hours, or until soft and cooked through. 5. Drain and serve.
**Per Serving:** Calories 222; Fat 11g; Sodium 314mg; Carbs 6g; Fiber 4g; Sugar 1g; Protein 12g

## Cheesy Spring Vegetable Pasta

Prep time: 15 minutes | Cook time: 7 hours 20 minutes | Serves: 8

4 cups baby carrots
1 cup sliced celery
1 (28-ounce) can diced tomatoes, drained
1 medium yellow onion, diced
2 cups fresh green beans, cut into 2-inch pieces
2 (15-ounce) cans cannellini beans, drained and rinsed
3 tablespoons minced garlic
6 cups Savory Vegetable Broth or store-bought broth
2 tablespoons Italian spicing
½ teaspoon sea salt, plus more for spicing
½ teaspoon ground black pepper, plus more for spicing
1 cup whole-grain elbow pasta
¾ to 1 cup grated Parmesan cheese, for topping

1. In a slow cooker, combine the carrots, celery, tomatoes, onion, green beans, cannellini beans, garlic, broth, Italian spicing, salt, and black pepper. Mix well. 2. Cover the slow cooker, cook on low temp setting for 7 hours, until the beans are easily mashed. 3. Remove the lid and stir in the pasta. Spiced with salt and pepper. Replace the lid and cook for an additional 15 to 20 minutes, until the pasta is tender. 4. Top with cheese, and serve the soup warm.
**Per Serving:** Calories 191; Fat 6g; Sodium 298mg; Carbs 1.4g; Fiber 0.3g; Sugar 0.1g; Protein 31.2g

## Garlic, Spinach and Beans Chili

Prep time: 15 minutes | Cook time: 6-8 hours | Serves: 8

2 tablespoons extra-virgin olive oil
¼ cup minced garlic
½ teaspoon onion powder
½ teaspoon garlic powder
1 tablespoon ground cumin
1 teaspoon chili powder
½ teaspoon paprika
1 medium yellow onion, chopped
2 (15-ounce) cans great northern beans, drained and rinsed
3 cups Savory Vegetable Broth or store-bought vegetable broth
1 (10-ounce) package frozen chopped spinach
Sea salt
Ground black pepper
1 cup shredded mild Cheddar cheese, for topping
1 cup sour cream, for topping
Fresh cilantro, for topping
Freshly squeezed lime juice, for topping

1. In a slow cooker, combine the olive oil, garlic, onion powder, garlic powder, cumin, chili powder, and paprika. Cook on high temp setting, stirring occasionally, for 2 to 3 minutes, until fragrant. 2. Add the onion and beans, then pour the broth over everything. Mix well. 3. Gently layer the spinach over the top. Do not mix; let the spinach stay on top to steam. 4. Cover, reduce the heat to low, and cook for 6 to 8 hours until the beans are soft and easily mashed. 5. Spiced with salt and black pepper. Stir the spinach into the chili. 6. Top with any combination of cheese; sour cream; chopped cilantro; or lime juice. Serve warm.
**Per Serving:** Calories 270; Fat 15g; Sodium 411mg; Carbs 5g; Fiber 3g; Sugar 2g; Protein 9g

## Mashed Root Vegetables

**Prep time: 15 minutes | Cook time: 6-7 hours | Serves: 8**

1 tablespoon butter
1 tablespoon extra-virgin olive oil
2 tablespoons minced garlic
1 teaspoon sea salt
½ teaspoon ground black pepper
1½ teaspoons dried thyme
2 pounds mixed root vegetables (any combination of sweet potatoes, white potatoes, carrots, turnips, and parsnips), peeled and chopped
¼ cup Savory Vegetable Broth or store-bought vegetable broth
⅓ cup 2 percent milk, whole milk, or half-and-half
Sliced scallions, for topping
¾ to 1 cup sour cream, for topping

1. In a slow cooker, combine the butter, olive oil, garlic, salt, black pepper, and thyme. Cook on high, stirring frequently, for 2 to 3 minutes, until fragrant. 2. Add the root vegetables, broth, and milk. Mix well. Cover the slow cooker and cook on low temp setting for 6 to 7 hours until the root vegetables are easily mashed. 3. Mash coarsely using a hand masher, or transfer to a blender and puree. 4. Serve the vegetables warm, topped with scallions and 2 tablespoons of sour cream per serving.
**Per Serving:** Calories 93; Fat 6.6g; Sodium 277mg; Carbs 1g; Fiber 0.2g; Sugar 0g; Protein 7.7g

## Udon Noodle Soup with Veggie

**Prep time: 15 minutes | Cook time: 6 hours | Serves: 4**

2 tablespoons extra-virgin olive oil
2 scallions, both white and green parts, chopped
1 tablespoon chopped peeled fresh ginger
2 tablespoons minced garlic
1 cup sliced shiitake mushrooms
2 tablespoons low-sodium soy sauce or coconut aminos
6 cups Savory Vegetable Broth or store-bought vegetable broth
2 teaspoons red or white miso
1 cup chopped bok choy
8 to 10 ounces dried udon
Fresh spinach and shredded carrots, for topping

1. In a slow cooker, combine the olive oil, scallions, ginger, garlic, mushrooms, and soy sauce. Cook on high, stirring frequently, for 2 to 3 minutes, until fragrant. 2. Pour in the broth and stir. 3. Add the miso and stir until dissolved. 4. Add the bok choy and udon. Mix). Cover and reduce the heat to low. Cook for 6 hours, until the udon is cooked. 5. Serve the noodle soup warm over a handful of fresh spinach and a handful of shredded carrots.
**Per Serving:** Calories 216; Fat 11g; Sodium 230mg; Carbs 5g; Fiber 3g; Sugar 1g; Protein 9g

## Collard Greens with Bacon

**Prep time: 15 minutes | Cook time: 7 hours | Serves: 10**

3 tablespoons extra-virgin olive oil
8 bacon slices, chopped
1 cup chopped or diced cooked ham
3 cups Savory Chicken Broth or store-bought chicken broth
1 tablespoon coconut sugar
2 tablespoons apple cider vinegar
¼ teaspoon red pepper flakes
8 cups (2 pounds) collard greens, ribs and stems removed, torn into bite-size pieces
Sea salt
Ground black pepper

1. Pour the olive oil into a slow cooker, then add the bacon. Cook on high, stirring frequently, for 2 to 3 minutes, until the bacon is crackling. 2. Add the ham, broth, sugar, vinegar, and red pepper flakes. Stir and cook for an additional 2 to 3 minutes. 3. Add the collard greens 1 cup at a time, stirring and letting the piece's wilt with each addition. 4. Cover, reduce the heat to low, and cook for 7 hours, until the collard greens are soft and cooked through. 5. Spiced with salt and black pepper. Serve the greens warm.
**Per Serving:** Calories 230; Fat 15.9g; Sodium 300mg; Carbs 15.9g; Fiber 9.3g; Sugar 3g; Protein 10g

---

## Onion & Bell Pepper Stuffed Tomatoes

**Prep time: 20 minutes | Cook time: 7 hours | Serves: 6**

6 large tomatoes
1 red onion, finely chopped
1 yellow bell pepper, stemmed, seeded, and chopped
3 garlic cloves, minced
¾ cup low-sodium whole-wheat bread crumbs
1½ cups shredded Colby cheese
¼ cup finely chopped flat-leaf parsley
1 teaspoon dried thyme leaves
½ cup Roasted Vegetable Broth

1. Cut the tops off the tomatoes. With a serrated spoon, core the tomatoes, reserving the pulp. Set the tomatoes aside. 2. In a bowl, mix the onion, bell pepper, garlic, bread crumbs, cheese, parsley, thyme, and reserved tomato pulp. 3. Stuff this mixture into the tomatoes, and place the tomatoes in a slow cooker. Pour the vegetable broth into the slow cooker. 4. Cover the slow cooker and cook on low temp setting for 6 to 7 hours, or until the tomatoes are tender.
**Per Serving:** Calories 271; Fat 14g; Sodium 288mg; Carbs 5g; Fiber 3g; Sugar 5g; Protein 11g

## Cheesy Potato Gratin

**Prep time: 20 minutes | Cook time: 7-9 hours | Serves: 8**

6 Yukon Gold potatoes, thinly sliced
2 onions, thinly sliced
4 garlic cloves, minced
3 tablespoons whole-wheat flour
4 cups 2% milk, divided

1½ cups Roasted Vegetable Broth
3 tablespoons melted butter
1 teaspoon dried thyme leaves
1½ cups shredded Havarti cheese

1. Grease a slow cooker with plain vegetable oil. 2. In the slow cooker, layer the potatoes, onions, and garlic. 3. In a bowl, mix the flour with ½ cup of the milk until well combined. Gradually add the milk, stirring with a wire whisk to avoid lumps. Stir in the vegetable broth, melted butter, and thyme leaves. 4. Pour the milk mixture over the potatoes in the slow cooker and top with the cheese. 5. Cover the slow cooker and cook on low temp setting for 7 to 9 hours, or until the potatoes are tender when pierced with a fork.
**Per Serving:** Calories 142; Fat 10.2g; Sodium 269mg; Carbs 4.9g; Fiber 2.7g; Sugar 2g; Protein 8.8g

## Roasted Vegetables

**Prep time: 20 minutes | Cook time: 6-8 hours | Serves: 8**

6 carrots, cut into 1-inch chunks
2 yellow onions, each cut into 8 wedges
2 sweet potatoes, peeled and cut into chunks
6 Yukon Gold potatoes, cut into chunks
8 whole garlic cloves, peeled

4 parsnips, peeled and cut into chunks
3 tablespoons olive oil
1 teaspoon dried thyme leaves
½ teaspoon salt
⅛ teaspoon freshly ground black pepper

1. In a slow cooker, mix all of the ingredients. 2. Cover the slow cooker and cook on low temp for 6 to 8 hours, or until the vegetables are tender.
**Per Serving:** Calories 220; Fat 13g; Sodium 321mg; Carbs 6g; Fiber 4g; Sugar 2g; Protein 12g

## Roasted butternut Squash Purée

**Prep time: 20 minutes | Cook time: 6-7 hours | Serves: 8**

1 (3-pound) butternut squash, peeled, seeded, and cut into 1-inch pieces
3 (1-pound) acorn squash, peeled, seeded, and cut into 1-inch pieces
2 onions, chopped
3 garlic cloves, minced
2 tablespoons olive oil
1 teaspoon dried marjoram leaves
½ teaspoon salt
⅛ teaspoon freshly ground black pepper

1. In a slow cooker, mix all of the ingredients. 2. Cover the slow cooker and cook on low temp setting for 6 to 7 hours, or until the squash is tender when pierced with a fork. 3. Use a potato masher to mash the squash right in the slow cooker.
**Per Serving:** Calories 226; Fat 9.3g; Sodium 324mg; Carbs 8.7g; Fiber 3g; Sugar 2g; Protein 12.6g

## Sweet & Sour Beets with Onions

**Prep time: 20 minutes | Cook time: 5-7 hours | Serves: 8**

10 medium beets, peeled and sliced
3 red onions, chopped
4 garlic cloves, minced
⅓ cup honey
⅓ cup lemon juice
1 cup water
2 tablespoons melted coconut oil
3 tablespoons cornstarch
½ teaspoon salt

1. In a slow cooker, mix the beets, onions, and garlic. 2. In a bowl, mix the honey, lemon juice, water, coconut oil, cornstarch, and salt until well combined. Pour this mixture over the beets. 3. Cover the slow cooker and cook on low temp setting for 5 to 7 hours, or until the beets are tender and the sauce has thickened.
**Per Serving:** Calories 221; Fat 9.4g; Sodium 321mg; Carbs 8.6g; Fiber 2g; Sugar 1g; Protein 14.2g

## Herbed Greens with Onions

### Prep time: 20 minutes | Cook time: 3-4 hours | Serves: 8

2 bunches Swiss chard, washed and cut into large pieces
2 bunches collard greens, washed and cut into large pieces
2 bunches kale, washed and cut into large pieces
3 onions, chopped
1½ cups Roasted Vegetable Broth
¼ cup honey
2 tablespoons lemon juice
1 teaspoon dried marjoram
1 teaspoon dried basil
¼ teaspoon salt

1. In a slow cooker, mix the Swiss chard, collard greens, kale, and onions. 2. In a bowl, mix the vegetable broth, honey, lemon juice, marjoram, basil, and salt. Pour into the slow cooker. 3. Cover the slow cooker and cook on low temp setting for 3 to 4 hours, or until the greens are very tender.
**Per Serving:** Calories 228; Fat 11.2g; Sodium 541mg; Carbs 10.3g; Fiber 4g; Sugar 2g; Protein 13.2g

## Delicious Turkey Stuffed Peppers

### Prep time: 5 minutes | Cook time: 6 hours | Serves: 4

1 lb. ground turkey
4 bell peppers, tops and seeds removed
1 onion, diced
1 jar (24 oz.) tomato sauce
Salt, pepper to taste

1. In a bowl combine the ground meat, onion and 2 tablespoon of pasta sauce. Stuff the peppers firmly. 2. Put the peppers into a slow cooker and cover with the pasta sauce. 3. Cover the slow cooker and cook for 6 hours on low temp setting.
**Per Serving:** Calories 224; Fat 12.3g; Sodium 458mg; Carbs 11.2g; Fiber 2g; Sugar 1g; Protein 14.2g

## Garlicky Mashed Red Potatoes

**Prep time: 15 minutes | Cook time: 4-5 hours | Serves: 14**

3 lb. small red potatoes
4 cloves garlic, finely chopped
2 tablespoons olive oil
1 teaspoon salt

½ cup water
½ cup of chives and onion cream cheese
¼ to ½ cup milk

1. Halve or quarter the potatoes. Place in slow cooker. Add garlic, oil, and salted water. Toss together. 2. Cover the slow cooker and cook on high temp for 3½ to 4½ hours or until potatoes are tender. 3. Using any beater mash potatoes and garlic. Blend cream cheese and milk into potatoes for soft consistency. 4. Serve immediately, or cover and hold in the slow cooker on low setting up to 2 hours.
**Per Serving:** Calories 242; Fat 13.1g; Sodium 269mg; Carbs 9.6g; Fiber 2g; Sugar 1g; Protein 14.2g

---

## Bacon Cabbage Casserole

**Prep time: 10 minutes | Cook time: 6 hours | Serves: 8**

1 small head of cabbage, cored, chopped
⅔ cup cooked, crumbled bacon
15 oz. pearl onions,

8 cups chicken broth
Salt, pepper to taste

1. Place the chopped cabbage into a slow cooker. 2. Top with onions and bacon. Spiced with salt and pepper. Pour the broth over the cabbage. 3. Close the lid and cook for 6 hours on high.
**Per Serving:** Calories 578; Fat 36g; Sodium 823mg; Carbs 49g; Fiber 5g; Sugar 6g; Protein 17g

# Chapter 3 Poultry

## Chicken Veggie Broth

**Prep time: 15 minutes | Cook time: 6-8 hours | Serves: 12**

1 chicken carcass
About 12 cups filtered water (enough to cover the bones)
2 carrots, roughly chopped
2 garlic cloves, roughly chopped
1 celery stalk, roughly chopped
½ onion, roughly chopped
2 bay leaves
1 parsley sprig
¾ teaspoon sea salt
½ teaspoon dried oregano
½ teaspoon dried basil leaves
1 tablespoon apple cider vinegar

1. In slow cooker, combine the chicken carcass, water, carrots, garlic, celery, onion, bay leaves, parsley, salt, oregano, basil, and vinegar. 2. Cover the slow cooker and set to low temp setting. Cook for 6 to 8 hours. 3. Skim off any scum from the surface of the broth, and pour the broth through a fine-mesh sieve into a bowl, discarding the chicken and veggie scraps.
**Per Serving:** Calories 195; Fat 4.9g; Sodium 110mg; Carbs 1.7g; Fiber 1g; Sugar 0.7g; Protein 33.4g

## Barbecued Chicken

**Prep time: 15 minutes | Cook time: 3 to 4 hours | Serves: 2**

4 to 5 boneless, skinless chicken breasts
2 cups Tangy Barbecue Sauce with Apple Cider Vinegar

1. In slow cooker, combine the chicken and barbecue sauce. Stir until the chicken breasts are well coated in the sauce. 2. Cover the slow cooker and set to high temp setting. Cook for 3 to 4 hours, or until the juices run clear. 3. Shred the chicken with a fork, mix it into the sauce, and serve.
**Per Serving:** Calories 208; Fat 12g; Sodium 145mg; Carbs 6.8g; Fiber 3.7g; Sugar 0.6g; Protein 17.5g

## Spicy Whole Chicken

**Prep time: 15 minutes | Cook time: 6-8 hours | Serves: 6**

- 1 teaspoon garlic powder
- 1 teaspoon chili powder
- 1 teaspoon paprika
- 1 teaspoon dried thyme leaves
- 1 teaspoon sea salt
- Pinch cayenne pepper
- Freshly ground black pepper
- 1 whole chicken (about 4 to 5 pounds), neck and giblets removed
- ½ medium onion, sliced

1. In a bowl, stir the garlic powder, chili powder, paprika, thyme, salt, and cayenne. Spiced with black pepper, and stir again to combine. Rub the spice mix all over the exterior of the chicken. 2. Place the chicken in the slow cooker with the sliced onion sprinkled around it. 3. Cover the slow cooker and set to low temp setting. Cook for 6 to 8 hours, or until the juices run clear, and serve.

**Per Serving:** Calories 285; Fat 12g; Sodium 541mg; Carbs 6g; Fiber 3g; Sugar 2g; Protein 16g

## Herbed Chicken with White Bean Stew

**Prep time: 15 minutes | Cook time: 8 hours | Serves: 8**

- 1½ pounds boneless chicken thighs (about 6 whole thighs)
- 1 pound (3½ cups) halved peeled fingerling or baby potatoes
- 2 cups baby carrots
- 1 medium onion, diced
- 1 cup chopped celery
- 2 cups chopped kale
- 2 (15-ounce) cans white cannellini beans, drained and rinsed
- 1 (14½-ounce) can diced tomatoes, drained
- 2 tablespoons minced garlic
- 1 bay leaf
- 2 teaspoons dried oregano
- 2 teaspoons dried thyme
- 2 teaspoons dried rosemary
- 4 cups Savory Chicken Broth or store-bought chicken broth
- Sea salt
- Ground black pepper
- ¾ to 1 cup grated Parmesan cheese, for topping

1. In a slow cooker, combine the chicken, potatoes, carrots, onion, celery, kale, beans, tomatoes, garlic, bay leaf, oregano, thyme, rosemary, and broth. 2. Mix well. Cover the slow cooker and cook on low temp setting for 8 hours, until the chicken has cooked through, the vegetables are soft, and the beans are easily mashed. 3. Remove the lid and remove the chicken. Shred using 2 forks. Return the meat to the slow cooker and stir. Spiced with salt and black pepper to taste. 4. Serve the stew warm, topped with 2 tablespoons of cheese per serving.

**Per Serving:** Calories 429; Fat 32.4g; Sodium 325mg; Carbs 5g; Fiber 1g; Sugar 3g; Protein 28g

## Healthy Salsa Chicken

**Prep time: 15 minutes | Cook time: 6-8 hours | Serves: 6**

4 to 5 boneless, skinless chicken breasts (about 2 pounds)
2 cups green salsa
1 cup chicken broth
2 tablespoons freshly squeezed lime juice
1 teaspoon sea salt
1 teaspoon chili powder

1. In slow cooker, combine the chicken, salsa, broth, lime juice, salt, and chili powder. Stir to combine. 2. Cover the slow cooker and set to low temp setting. Cook for 6 to 8 hours, or until the juices run clear. 3. Shred the chicken with a fork, mix it into the sauce, and serve.
**Per Serving:** Calories 112; Fat 2g; Sodium 12mg; Carbs 8g; Fiber 1g; Sugar 6g; Protein 0g

## Thai Chicken Curry

**Prep time: 15 minutes | Cook time: 7 hours | Serves: 8**

3 cups Savory Chicken Broth
5 tablespoons red Thai curry paste, such as Mae Ploy or Thai Kitchen
2⅔ cups canned coconut milk
1 tablespoon coconut sugar
1½ tablespoons low-sodium soy sauce or coconut aminos
1½ tablespoons minced fresh ginger
1 tablespoon fish sauce
¼ cup minced garlic
1½ pounds boneless, skinless chicken thighs, cut into bite-size pieces
1½ cups diced carrots
1 medium yellow onion, chopped
1 large red bell pepper, cored and sliced
2 cups chopped kale
1½ to 2 cups cooked basmati rice or cauliflower rice
Chopped fresh cilantro, freshly squeezed lime juice, or sliced chiles of choice (such as Thai chiles or jalapeños), for topping

1. In a slow cooker, combine the broth, curry paste, coconut milk, sugar, soy sauce, ginger, fish sauce, garlic, chicken, carrots, and onion. 2. Cover the slow cooker and cook on low temp setting for 6 hours, until the chicken has cooked through and the vegetables are soft. 3. Remove the lid and add the bell pepper and kale. Replace the lid and cook for an additional 45 minutes to 1 hour. 4. Serve the curry warm over the rice with cilantro, lime juice, or chiles.
**Per Serving:** Calories 311; Fat 6g; Sodium 112mg; Carbs 15g; Fiber 6g; Sugar 12g; Protein 2g

## Sweet Garlic Chicken and Carrots

Prep time: 15 minutes | Cook time: 7 hours 45 minutes | Serves: 10

1 cup low-sodium soy sauce or coconut aminos
¾ cup honey
2 teaspoons minced garlic
¼ cup tomato paste
2 to 3 tablespoons apple cider vinegar
2 tablespoons extra-virgin olive oil
5 boneless, skinless chicken breasts
3 cups baby carrots
1 small white onion, chopped
1 teaspoon sea salt
1 teaspoon ground black pepper
20 ounces fresh green beans, trimmed
2 tablespoons chopped fresh parsley, for topping

1. In a bowl, whisk the soy sauce, honey, garlic, tomato paste, and vinegar. 2. Grease a slow cooker with the olive oil. 3. Add the chicken, carrots, onion, salt, black pepper, and soy sauce mixture. Mix well. Cover the slow cooker and cook on low temp setting for 7 hours, until the chicken has cooked through. 4. Remove the lid and add the green beans. Mix well. Replace the lid and cook for an additional 30 to 45 minutes, until the green beans are tender. 5. Sprinkle the parsley over the top, and serve warm.

**Per Serving:** Calories 173; Fat 13.6g; Sodium 281mg; Carbs 3g; Fiber 1g; Sugar 1g; Protein 10g

## Chicken Strips with Tomatoes

Prep time: 20 minutes | Cook time: 4-6 hours | Serves: 8

2 onions, chopped
6 garlic cloves, minced
4 large tomatoes, seeded and chopped
2 dried red chilies, crushed
1 jalapeño pepper, minced
2 tablespoons chili powder
3 tablespoons cocoa powder
2 tablespoons coconut sugar
½ cup Chicken Stock
6 (5-ounce) boneless, skinless chicken breasts

1. In a slow cooker, mix the onions, garlic, tomatoes, chili peppers, and jalapeño peppers. 2. In a bowl, mix the chili powder, cocoa powder, coconut sugar, and chicken stock. 3. Cut the chicken breasts into 1-inch strips crosswise and add to the slow cooker. Pour the chicken stock mixture over all. 4. Cover the slow cooker and cook on low temp setting for 4 to 6 hours. 5. Serve with toothpicks or little plates and forks.

**Per Serving:** Calories 152; Fat 50g; Sodium 438mg; Carbs 7g; Fiber 0g; Sugar 7g; Protein 132g

## Spicy Chicken with Greens

Prep time: 20 minutes | Cook time: 6-8 hours | Serves: 8

- 2 (16-ounce) packages prepared collard greens
- 2 cups chopped kale
- 2 onions, chopped
- 6 garlic cloves, minced
- 2 red chili peppers, minced
- 1 lemongrass stalk
- 10 (4-ounce) boneless, skinless chicken thighs
- 1 cup Chicken Stock
- 1 cup canned coconut milk
- 3 tablespoons freshly squeezed lime juice

1. In a slow cooker, mix the greens and kale and top with the onions, garlic, chili peppers, lemongrass, and chicken. Pour the chicken stock and coconut milk over all. 2. Cover the slow cooker and cook on low temp setting for 6 to 8 hours, or until the chicken and the greens are tender. 3. Stir in the lime juice and serve.

**Per Serving:** Calories 134; Fat 9.8g; Sodium 394mg; Carbs 2g; Fiber 0g; Sugar 1g; Protein 9g

---

## Roasted Fennel Chicken and Squash

Prep time: 20 minutes | Cook time: 6-8 hours | Serves: 8

- 1 (3-pound) butternut squash, peeled, seeded, and cut into 1-inch pieces
- 2 (1-pound) acorn squash, peeled, seeded, and cut into 1-inch pieces
- 2 fennel bulbs, cored and sliced
- 1 (8-ounce) package cremini mushrooms, sliced
- 8 (6-ounce) bone-in, skinless chicken breasts
- 3 sprigs fresh thyme
- 1 bay leaf
- 1 cup chicken stock
- ½ cup canned coconut milk
- 2 tablespoons lemon juice

1. In a slow cooker, mix the butternut squash, acorn squash, fennel, mushrooms, chicken, thyme, bay leaf, chicken stock, and coconut milk. 2. Cover the slow cooker and cook on low temp setting for 6 to 8 hours. Stir in the lemon juice and serve.

**Per Serving:** Calories 227; Fat 9.8g; Sodium 525mg; Carbs 7g; Fiber 2g; Sugar 4g; Protein 28g

## Southwest Chicken with Zucchini

Prep time: 15 minutes | Cook time: 6 hours | Serves: 6

4 chicken breasts, with boneless, skinless, halved
1 zucchini, chopped
1 bell pepper, cubed

1 jar salsa, sugar free
Salt, pepper to taste

1. In a bowl stir the chicken breasts in salsa. Put all the ingredients into the slow cooker. Flavor with salt and pepper. Close the lid. 2. Cook for 6 hours on low temp setting.
**Per Serving:** Calories 248; Fat 21.1g; Sodium 429mg; Carbs 2g; Fiber 0g; Sugar 1g; Protein 12g

## Cheesy Salsa Chicken

Prep time: 5 minutes | Cook time: 6 hours | Serves: 4

4 chicken breasts, boneless, skinless, halved
2 cups salsa
1 cup low-fat Mozzarella, grated

1-2 tablespoon lemon juice
Salt, pepper to taste

1. In a saucepan, simmer 2 cups of salsa until it is reduced to 1 cup. Put the chicken in the slow cooker in a single layer. 2. Spiced with salt, pepper. Add lemon juice to salsa and pour the mixture over the chicken. 3. Cover the slow cooker and cook for 6 hours on high. Open the lid and sprinkle the chicken with grated Mozzarella. 4. Then cook for 5 min or until the cheese melts.
**Per Serving:** Calories 509; Fat 40.6g; Sodium 525mg; Carbs 8g; Fiber 2g; Sugar 5g; Protein 28g

## Chicken Noodle with Colorful Veggies

Prep time: 10 minutes | Cook time: 30 minutes | Serves: 6

2 teaspoons butter
1 cup sliced celery
1 cup chopped carrots
½ cup chopped onion
½ teaspoon thyme
1 teaspoon poultry spicing

2 (32-ounce) containers plus one 14 oz. can of chicken broth
2 teaspoons chicken bouillon granules
8 oz. egg noodles
2 cups cooked chicken
Parsley

1. Melt butter in a slow cooker. Sauté the celery, carrots and onion for 5 to 10 minutes. Add thyme, poultry spicing, chicken broth and bouillon. 2. Bring to a boil. Fill in noodles and chicken, and cook on low temp setting for 20 minutes. Sprinkle with parsley.
**Per Serving:** Calories 138; Fat 10.6g; Sodium 102mg; Carbs 1g; Fiber 0g; Sugar 1g; Protein 9g

## Chicken Chili with Beans

Prep time: 15 minutes | Cook time: 7 hours 30 minutes | Serves: 6

2 pounds boneless, skinless chicken breasts, cut into 1-inch pieces
1 medium sweet onion, finely chopped
1 medium green bell pepper, finely chopped
1 tablespoon minced garlic
2 (14½-ounce) cans no-salt-added diced tomatoes, with their juices
¾ cup picante sauce

1 teaspoon chili powder
1 teaspoon ground cumin
¼ teaspoon kosher salt
1 (15 to 16-ounce) can no-salt-added black beans, drained and rinsed
Shredded cheddar cheese, for serving
Thinly sliced scallions, green and white parts, for serving
Diced avocado, for serving

1. In a slow cooker, combine the chicken, onion, bell pepper, garlic, tomatoes with their juices, picante sauce, chili powder, cumin, and salt. 2. Cover the slow cooker and cook on low temp setting for 6 to 7 hours, until the chicken is no longer pink inside. Stir in the beans and cook an additional 30 minutes, until the beans are warm. 3. Spoon into serving bowls and top with cheese, scallions, and avocado.
**Per Serving:** Calories 293; Fat 13.8g; Sodium 855mg; Carbs 28g; Fiber 8g; Sugar 11g; Protein 19g

## Sweet & Spicy Turkey Salad

**Prep time: 5 minutes | Cook time: 4 hours | Serves: 8**

1 cup cayenne pepper hot sauce
¼ cup honey
¼ cup low-sodium gluten-free tamari or soy sauce
2 to 3 pounds turkey tenderloin
2 teaspoons garlic pepper or freshly ground black pepper
1 teaspoon onion powder

Torn romaine lettuce leaves, for serving
Grated carrots, for serving
Chopped celery, for serving
Crumbled blue cheese, for serving
Blue cheese or ranch dressing, for serving

1. In a slow cooker, whisk the hot sauce, honey, and tamari. Rub the turkey all over with the garlic pepper and onion powder and place it in the slow cooker in a single layer. Roll the turkey in the sauce to Grease all sides. 2. Cover the slow cooker and cook on low temp setting for 3 to 4 hours, until the turkey is cooked through and shreds easily. Transfer the turkey to a cutting board and shred, using 2 forks. 3. Place the lettuce on serving plates or in pasta bowls. Top with the turkey, carrots, celery, and blue cheese. 4. Drizzle on about 1 tablespoon of sauce from the slow cooker per plate, if desired, and add the salad dressing. Serve immediately.
**Per Serving:** Calories 151; Fat 7.5g; Sodium 621mg; Carbs 20g; Fiber 5g; Sugar 2g; Protein 5g

## Garlicky Turkey Breasts

**Prep time: 15 minutes | Cook time: 6 hours | Serves: 12**

7 lb. turkey breasts, no bones
4 cloves garlic, sliced
½ cup water

1 tablespoon yacón syrup
Salt, pepper to taste

1. Put all the ingredients into the slow cooker. Make sure all turkey pieces are evenly Greased. 2. Cook for 6 hours on low temp setting.
**Per Serving:** Calories 288; Fat 23.3g; Sodium 308mg; Carbs 6g; Fiber 1g; Sugar 5g; Protein 14g

## Delicious Chicken Meatloaf

Prep time: 15 minutes | Cook time: 6 hours | Serves: 8

¼ cup 2% milk

1 large egg

½ cup bread crumbs

1 tablespoon Worcestershire sauce

¼ teaspoon kosher salt

1 teaspoon stone-ground mustard

¼ teaspoon freshly ground black pepper

1 tablespoon minced garlic

1 small green bell pepper, finely chopped

1 small yellow onion, finely chopped

2 pounds ground chicken or turkey

½ cup Louisiana-style barbecue sauce

1. Tear off a piece of aluminum foil long enough to go partway up the sides of a slow cooker. Place it in the slow cooker, mold it to fit, and then transfer it to a work surface. 2. In a bowl, combine the milk, egg, bread crumbs, Worcestershire sauce, salt, Creole-style mustard, black pepper, garlic, bell pepper, and onion. Use hands to mix in the chicken until just combined. 3. In the center of the foil, form the meat into an oval-shape loaf. Lift the loaf using the foil and place it in the slow cooker. Top with the barbecue sauce. 4. Cover the slow cooker and cook on low temp setting for 5 to 6 hours, until the meatloaf is cooked through. Use the foil to lift the meatloaf out of the slow cooker and onto a cutting board. Discard the juices. 5. Let the meatloaf rest for 10 minutes, then slice and serve immediately.
**Per Serving:** Calories 217; Fat 21.8g; Sodium 207mg; Carbs 7g; Fiber 4g; Sugar 3g; Protein 2g

## Herbed Chicken and Cherry Tomatoes

Prep time: 15 minutes | Cook time: 5-7 hours | Serves: 4

3 pounds boneless, skinless chicken thighs

½ cup low-sodium chicken broth

2 cups cherry tomatoes, halved

4 garlic cloves, minced

2 teaspoons garlic salt

¼ teaspoon ground white pepper

2 tablespoons chopped fresh basil

2 tablespoons chopped fresh oregano

1. Combine all the ingredients in the slow cooker and mix well. 2. Cover the slow cooker and cook on low temp setting for 5 to 7 hours.
**Per Serving:** Calories 268; Fat 13.6g; Sodium 348mg; Carbs 1.2g; Fiber 0.2g; Sugar 0.6g; Protein 35.2g

## Aromatic Chicken Cacciatore

**Prep time: 15 minutes | Cook time: 5-7 hours | Serves: 4**

1 (15-ounce) can crushed tomatoes
8 ounces mushrooms, sliced
2 red or green bell peppers, seeded and sliced
2 carrots, peeled and chopped
1 onion, sliced
3 garlic cloves, minced
½ cup low-sodium chicken broth or water
2 teaspoons dried oregano
2 teaspoons dried basil
1 teaspoon salt
1 teaspoon freshly ground black pepper
3 pounds boneless, skinless chicken thighs

1. Combine the crushed tomatoes, mushrooms, bell peppers, carrots, onion, garlic, broth, and spicing in the slow cooker and mix well. 2. Add the chicken and mix again. 3. Cover the slow cooker and cook on low temp setting for 5 to 7 hours.
**Per Serving:** Calories 326; Fat 19.6g; Sodium 458mg; Carbs 1.9g; Fiber 0.4g; Sugar 0.6g; Protein 35.6g

## Garlic-Citrus Chicken with Potatoes

**Prep time: 15 minutes | Cook time: 5-7 hours | Serves: 4**

1 onion, sliced
1 pound red potatoes, diced
2 pounds boneless, skinless chicken thighs
⅓ cup freshly squeezed lime juice
¼ cup freshly squeezed orange juice
2 tablespoons extra-virgin olive oil
7 garlic cloves, minced
1 teaspoon salt
1 teaspoon dried oregano
¼ teaspoon ground cumin
1 lemon, sliced
1 jalapeño, seeded and sliced

1. Combine the onion and potatoes in the slow cooker. Add the chicken on top. 2. In a bowl, whisk the lime juice, orange juice, oil, garlic, salt, oregano, and cumin. 3. Pour the sauce on top of all the ingredients in the slow cooker. Top with the sliced lemon and jalapeño. 4. Cover the slow cooker and cook on low temp setting for 5 to 7 hours.
**Per Serving:** Calories 150; Fat 6.7g; Sodium 336mg; Carbs 1.9g; Fiber 0.2g; Sugar 0.1g; Protein 19.6g

# Chapter 4 Pork, Beef, and Lamb

## Classic Beef Bones Broth

**Prep time: 15 minutes | Cook time: 24 hours | Serves: 4**

2 pounds beef marrow bones
2 cups roughly chopped onions, celery, carrots, garlic, or scraps
2 bay leaves
1 tablespoon apple cider vinegar
Filtered water, to cover the ingredients

1. In slow cooker, combine the bones, onion, celery, carrots, garlic, bay leaves, and vinegar. Add enough water to cover the ingredients. 2. Cover the slow cooker and set to low temp setting. Cook for 18 to 24 hours. The longer it cooks, the more nutrients you get from the bones and vegetables. 3. Skim off and discard any foam from the surface. Ladle the broth through a fine-mesh sieve or cheesecloth into a bowl. Transfer to airtight containers to store.
**Per Serving:** Calories 288; Fat 23.3g; Sodium 308mg; Carbs 6g; Fiber 1g; Sugar 5g; Protein 14g

## Beef Bolognese

**Prep time: 15 minutes | Cook time: 7-8 hours | Serves: 6**

1 tablespoon extra-virgin olive oil
3 garlic cloves, minced
½ cup chopped onion
⅔ cup chopped celery
⅔ cup chopped carrot
1-pound ground beef
1 (14-ounce) can diced tomatoes
1 tablespoon white wine vinegar
⅛ teaspoon ground nutmeg
2 bay leaves
½ teaspoon red pepper flakes
Dash sea salt
Dash freshly ground black pepper

1. Grease the slow cooker with the olive oil. 2. Add the garlic, onion, celery, carrot, ground beef, tomatoes, vinegar, nutmeg, bay leaves, red pepper flakes, salt, and black pepper. 3. Using a fork, break up the ground beef as much as possible. Cover the slow cooker and set to low temp setting. Cook for 7 to 8 hours. 4. Remove and discard the bay leaves. Stir, breaking up the meat completely, and serve.
**Per Serving:** Calories 138; Fat 10.6g; Sodium 102mg; Carbs 1g; Fiber 0g; Sugar 1g; Protein 9g

## Beef Meatballs with Tomatoes

### Prep time: 15 minutes | Cook time: 7-8 hours | Serves: 4

1½ pounds ground beef
1 large egg
1 small white onion, minced
¼ cup minced mushrooms
1 teaspoon garlic powder
½ teaspoon sea salt

½ teaspoon dried oregano
¼ teaspoon freshly ground black pepper
¼ teaspoon ground ginger
Dash red pepper flakes
1 (14-ounce) can crushed tomatoes

1. In a bowl, combine the ground beef, egg, onion, mushrooms, garlic powder, salt, oregano, black pepper, ginger, and red pepper flakes. Mix well. Form the beef mixture into about 12 meatballs. 2. Pour the tomatoes into slow cooker. Gently arrange the meatballs on top. 3. Cover the slow cooker and set to low temp setting. Cook for 7 to 8 hours and serve.
**Per Serving:** Calories 293; Fat 13.8g; Sodium 855mg; Carbs 28g; Fiber 8g; Sugar 11g; Protein 19g

## Pork and Pumpkin Stew

### Prep time: 15 minutes | Cook time: 5 hours 40 minutes | Serves: 8

1 tablespoon extra-virgin olive oil
1-pound ground pork
1 large yellow onion, diced
1 (16-ounce) can pumpkin puree
2½ cups Savory Chicken Broth
2 tablespoons minced garlic

½ teaspoon ground cinnamon
1 bay leaf
2 cups 2 percent milk
Sea salt
Ground black pepper

1. Grease a slow cooker with the olive oil. 2. Set the heat to high. Add the pork and cook, continuously stirring and breaking up the meat, for 2 to 3 minutes. 3. Add the onion, pumpkin, broth, garlic, cinnamon, and bay leaf. Mix well. Cover the slow cooker and cook on low temp setting for 5 hours, until the pork has cooked through. 4. Remove the lid and stir in the milk. Replace the lid and cook for an additional 30 to 40 minutes, until heated through. 5. Spiced with salt and black pepper. Serve the stew warm.
**Per Serving:** Calories 151; Fat 7.5g; Sodium 621mg; Carbs 20g; Fiber 5g; Sugar 2g; Protein 5g

## Moroccan-style Lamb Shanks

**Prep time: 15 minutes | Cook time: 5-6 hours | Serves: 8**

- 2 tablespoons extra-virgin olive oil
- 1 large white onion, diced
- 1 teaspoon minced garlic
- 1 tablespoon ground cumin
- 2 teaspoons ground coriander
- 1 teaspoon ground turmeric
- 1 teaspoon paprika
- 1 tablespoon minced fresh ginger
- ½ teaspoon ground cinnamon
- 1 teaspoon sea salt
- 1 teaspoon ground black pepper
- 6 or 7 lamb shanks, trimmed of excess fat
- 4 cups savory chicken broth
- 1 large sweet potato, peeled and chopped
- 1 (15-ounce) can chickpeas, drained and rinsed
- 1 cup dried apricots
- 2 medium tomatoes, peeled and chopped
- ¾ to 1 cup feta cheese, for topping
- Arugula, for topping

1. Grease a slow cooker with the olive oil. 2. Set the heat to high. Add the onion and cook for 2 to 3 minutes, until fragrant. 3. Meanwhile, in a bowl, combine the garlic, cumin, coriander, turmeric, paprika, ginger, cinnamon, salt, and black pepper. 4. Thoroughly Grease each lamb shank with the spice mixture, and add them to the slow cooker. Sear for 2 to 3 minutes per side. 5. Add the broth, spice mixture, the sweet potato, chickpeas, apricots, and tomatoes. Mix well. 6. Cover, reduce the heat to low, and cook for 5 to 6 hours, until the lamb shanks have cooked through. 7. Top with 2 tablespoons of cheese per serving and arugula. Serve the lamb warm.

**Per Serving:** Calories 217; Fat 21.8g; Sodium 207mg; Carbs 7g; Fiber 4g; Sugar 3g; Protein 2g

## Gingered Pork Chops with Carrots

**Prep time: 20 minutes | Cook time: 6-8 hours | Serves: 8**

- 2 onions, chopped
- 3 garlic cloves, minced
- 4 large carrots, peeled and cut into chunks
- 8 (5-ounce) pork chops
- 3 tablespoons grated fresh ginger root
- 3 tablespoons honey
- ½ cup chicken stock
- ½ teaspoon ground ginger
- ½ teaspoon salt
- ⅛ teaspoon freshly ground black pepper

1. In a slow cooker, mix the onions, garlic, and carrots. Top with the pork chops. 2. In a bowl, mix the ginger root, honey, stock, ginger, salt, and pepper. Pour into the slow cooker. 3. Cover the slow cooker and cook on low temp setting for 6 to 8 hours, or until the pork is very tender.

**Per Serving:** Calories 80; Fat 6g; Sodium 444mg; Carbs 6g; Fiber 1g; Sugar 4g; Protein 1g

## Beef Roast with Vegetables

**Prep time: 15 minutes | Cook time: 9-10 hours | Serves: 8**

2 tablespoons extra-virgin olive oil
4 medium potatoes, peeled and diced
5 large carrots, sliced
1 medium yellow onion, diced
1 teaspoon minced garlic
4 pounds beef chuck roast
1 teaspoon sea salt
1 teaspoon ground black pepper
2½ cups beef broth
1½ tablespoons Worcestershire sauce
1 teaspoon dried basil
3 tablespoons cornstarch
Chopped fresh parsley, for topping

1. In a slow cooker, combine the olive oil, potatoes, carrots, onion, and garlic. Cook on high, stirring occasionally, for 3 to 4 minutes, until the vegetables begin to sizzle. 2. Meanwhile, spiced the beef with the salt and black pepper. Place on top of the vegetables in the slow cooker. 3. In a bowl, combine the broth, Worcestershire sauce, and basil. Mix well. 4. Pour the mixture into the slow cooker. Cover, reduce the heat to low, and cook for 9 to 10 hours, until the beef is easily shredded and the vegetables are very soft. 5. Remove the lid and transfer ½ cup of the liquid from the slow cooker to a bowl. 6. Whisk the cornstarch into the bowl until the mixture has thickened. Then, mix the slurry back into the ingredients in the slow cooker, making sure it is well combined with the vegetables and liquid. 7. Replace the lid and cook for an additional 2 to 3 minutes, until the gravy has thickened. 8. Transfer the beef and vegetables to a serving platter. 9. Pour the gravy over the beef and garnish with parsley. Serve warm.
**Per Serving:** Calories 23; Fat 1.3g; Sodium 40mg; Carbs 2g; Fiber 1g; Sugar 1g; Protein 1g

## Beef Pot Roast

**Prep time: 20 minutes | Cook time: 8-10 hours | Serves: 8**

8 Yukon Gold potatoes, cut into chunks
4 large carrots, peeled and cut into chunks
2 onions, chopped
1 leek, sliced
8 garlic cloves, sliced
1 (3-pound) grass-fed chuck shoulder roast or tri-tip roast
1 teaspoon dried marjoram
½ teaspoon salt
¼ teaspoon freshly ground black pepper
1 cup beef stock

1. In a slow cooker, mix the potatoes, carrots, onions, leek, and garlic. 2. Place the beef on top of the vegetables and sprinkle with the marjoram, salt, and pepper. 3. Pour the beef stock into the slow cooker. 4. Cover the slow cooker and cook on low temp setting for 8 to 10 hours, or until the beef is very tender. 5. Serve the beef with the vegetables.
**Per Serving:** Calories 104; Fat 2.5g; Sodium 29mg; Carbs 18g; Fiber 4g; Sugar 2g; Protein 3g

## Delicious Beef Stroganoff

**Prep time: 20 minutes | Cook time: 9 ½ hours | Serves: 8**

2 onions, chopped
2 cups sliced cremini mushrooms
5 large carrots, sliced
8 garlic cloves, sliced
2½ pounds grass-fed chuck shoulder roast, trimmed of fat and cut in 2-inch cubes
2 cups beef stock
3 tablespoons mustard
1 bay leaf
1 teaspoon dried marjoram
1½ cups sour cream
3 tablespoons cornstarch

1. In a slow cooker, mix the onions, mushrooms, carrots, garlic, and beef. 2. In a bowl, mix the beef stock and mustard. Add the bay leaf and marjoram and pour into the slow cooker. 3. Cover the slow cooker and cook on low temp setting for 7 to 9 hours, or until the beef is very tender. 4. In a bowl, mix the sour cream and cornstarch. Add 1 cup of the liquid from the slow cooker and whisk until well blended. 5. Add the sour cream mixture to the slow cooker. Cover the slow cooker and cook on low temp setting for 20 to 30 minutes, or until the liquid has thickened. 6. Serve.
**Per Serving:** Calories 134; Fat 2.8g; Sodium 64mg; Carbs 26g; Fiber 4g; Sugar 8g; Protein 3g

## Beef with Bean Burrito Casserole

**Prep time: 20 minutes | Cook time: 5-7 hours | Serves: 8**

1½ pounds grass-fed lean ground beef
2 onions, chopped
4 garlic cloves, minced
2 jalapeño peppers, minced
1 (16-ounce) no-salt-added vegetarian refried beans
1 (15-ounce) no-salt-added black beans, drained and rinsed
1 tablespoon chili powder
1 teaspoon dried oregano
8 corn tortillas
2 cups shredded white Cheddar cheese

1. In saucepan, cook the beef, onions, and garlic over medium-high heat for 8 to 10 minutes, stirring to break up the meat. Drain well. 2. Add the jalapeño peppers, refried beans, black beans, chili powder, and oregano to the beef mixture. 3. In a slow cooker, layer the beef mixture with the tortillas and shredded cheese. 4. Cover the slow cooker and cook on low temp setting for 5 to 7 hours, or until the tortillas have softened.
**Per Serving:** Calories 153; Fat 2.8g; Sodium 28mg; Carbs 26g; Fiber 1g; Sugar 1g; Protein 6g

## Herbed Pork Loin with Dried Fruit and Leeks

**Prep time: 20 minutes | Cook time: 7-9 hours | Serves: 8**

2 leeks, sliced
1 cup dried apricots
1 cup dried pears, sliced
½ cup golden raisins
1 (3-pound) boneless pork loin
½ teaspoon salt
1 teaspoon dried thyme leaves
1 cup apricot nectar

1. In a slow cooker, place the leeks, apricots, pears, and raisins. Top with the pork. Sprinkle the pork with the salt and thyme. 2. Pour the apricot nectar around the pork, over the fruit. 3. Cover the slow cooker and cook on low temp setting for 7 to 9 hours.
**Per Serving:** Calories 292; Fat 24.3g; Sodium 660mg; Carbs 5g; Fiber 0g; Sugar 3g; Protein 14g

## Stuffed Peppers with Ground Beef and Rice

**Prep time: 25 minutes | Cook time: 1 hours 25 minutes | Serves: 6**

6 green or red bell peppers
1 tablespoon butter
1 tablespoon extra-virgin olive oil
½ cup chopped onion
½ cup chopped celery
1 can (14.5 oz.) diced tomatoes, undrained
1 can (8 ounces) tomato sauce
1 clove garlic, crushed
1 teaspoon dried oregano
½ teaspoon dried basil
2 teaspoon salt, divided
½ teaspoon ground black pepper, divided
1 egg, lightly beaten
1½ teaspoon Worcestershire sauce
1½ lb. lean ground beef
1½ cups cooked long-grain rice
shredded mild Cheddar cheese, about ½ to ¾ cup, optional

1. Cut the tops of the peppers off and remove seeds and pith. Place the peppers into a large pot with salted water. Boil, then reduce heat, cover, and simmer for 5 minutes. 2. In a preheated with olive oil skillet pan, sauté the chopped onion and chopped celery until the vegetables are tender. 3. Add the can of diced tomatoes, tomato sauce, crushed garlic, oregano, basil, 1 teaspoon salt, and ¼ teaspoon of black pepper. Simmer for about 10 minutes. 4. In a bowl, combine an egg with the 1 teaspoon of salt, ¼ teaspoon of black pepper, and Worcestershire sauce. Gently stir to blend. 5. Add the ground beef, cooked rice, and 1 cup of the tomato sauce mixture. Mix well. 6. Heat a slow cooker to 350°F. Stuff the ground beef mixture into the peppers and place them in a slow cooker. Pour the tomato mixture over the stuffed peppers. 7. Bake the peppers for about 45 minutes.
**Per Serving:** Calories 193; Fat 8.9g; Sodium 93mg; Carbs 2g; Fiber 1g; Sugar 0g; Protein 25g

## Beef Chili and Pinto Beans

**Prep time: 20 minutes | Cook time: 5 hours | Serves: 8**

- 2 lb. ground beef, 85% lean, or use part ground pork
- 1 cup chopped onion
- 3 cloves garlic, minced
- 4 oz. chopped green chili peppers
- 3 tablespoon minced jalapeño peppers
- 1 large can (28 oz.) crushed tomatoes
- 1 can (14.5 oz.) diced tomatoes
- 3 tablespoon tomato paste, about half of a 6-oz can
- 1 can (15 oz.) pinto beans, drained
- 3 tablespoon chili powder
- 1 teaspoon granulated sugar, optional
- ¾ teaspoon ground cumin
- ½ teaspoon red pepper
- ½ teaspoon freshly ground black pepper
- 1 teaspoon salt or to taste

1. In a skillet pan, brown the ground beef with the onion until no longer pink and the onion is tender. 2. Add garlic, the canned chili peppers and jalapeño peppers and cook for 3 minutes more, stirring. 3. Move to a slow cooker and add the crushed tomatoes, diced tomatoes, tomato paste, pinto beans, chili powder, sugar, cumin, red and black pepper, and salt, to taste. 4. Cover the slow cooker and cook on low temp setting for 5 to 6 hours or on high for 2 to 4 hours. 5. Serve with fresh baked buttermilk cornbread.

**Per Serving:** Calories 101; Fat 5.4g; Sodium 106mg; Carbs 8g; Fiber 3g; Sugar 3g; Protein 7g

---

## Pork Loin Roast with Potatoes

**Prep time: 15 minutes | Cook time: 8-9 hours | Serves: 6**

- 1 lb. small red potatoes, cut in half
- 1 lb. sweet potatoes, peeled and cut into chunks
- 2 red bell peppers, cut into large pieces
- 1 (3-lb) boneless pork loin roast
- ¼ cup Dijon mustard
- 1 teaspoon dried thyme
- ½ teaspoon salt
- ⅛ teaspoon black pepper
- 1½ cups low sodium beef broth

1. Place potatoes and bell peppers in a 4 to 5-quart slow cooker. In a bowl, mix mustard, thyme, salt, and black pepper and spread evenly over the pork. 2. Lay the pork out on top of the vegetables in the slow cooker and pour the beef broth over all. 3. Cover the slow cooker and cook on low temp setting for 8-9 hours. 4. Slice the pork and serve with the vegetables and juices.

**Per Serving:** Calories 147; Fat 7.3g; Sodium 56mg; Carbs 20g; Fiber 5g; Sugar 11g; Protein 4g

## Pulled Pork with Juicy Pineapple

**Prep time: 10 minutes | Cook time: 9 hours | Serves: 8**

1 (2½ to 3-pound) boneless pork butt, trimmed of visible fat
1 large sweet onion, finely chopped
1 (8-ounce) can pineapple tidbits or chunks, packed in juice
1½ cups Smoky Barbecue Sauce

1. In a slow cooker, place the pork. Scatter the onion all over the top of the pork. Pour in the pineapple with its juices, followed by the barbecue sauce. 2. Cover the slow cooker and cook on low temp setting for 8 to 9 hours, until the pork is tender. Using forks, shred the pork and mix it into the sauce. 3. Serve with additional barbecue sauce, if desired.
**Per Serving:** Calories 162; Fat 9.4g; Sodium 68mg; Carbs 21g; Fiber 4g; Sugar 16g; Protein 1g

## Pork and Celery with Mulled Cider

**Prep time: 10 minutes | Cook time: 10 hours | Serves: 6**

1 medium sweet onion, cut into 6 wedges
4 large carrots, cut into 1-inch pieces
1½ pounds celery root, peeled and cut into 1-inch pieces
1 (2 to 3-pound) boneless pork shoulder or butt, trimmed of visible fat
Kosher salt
Freshly ground black pepper
2 teaspoons paprika
1 teaspoon onion powder
½ teaspoon dried thyme
3 cups Mulled Apple Cider, apple cider, or unsweetened apple juice

1. In a slow cooker, combine the onion, carrots, and celery root. 2. Rub the pork all over with salt, pepper, the paprika, onion powder, and thyme, then place it on top of the vegetables in the slow cooker. Pour in the cider. 3. Cover the slow cooker and cook on low temp setting for 9 to 10 hours, until the pork is tender. 4. Pull the pork into large chunks and place it, along with the vegetables, on a serving platter. Drizzle with some of the sauce from the slow cooker.
**Per Serving:** Calories 271; Fat 9.3g; Sodium 15mg; Carbs 43g; Fiber 6g; Sugar 2g; Protein 5g

## Tropical Thai-Style Curry Pork Tenderloin

**Prep time: 15 minutes | Cook time: 7 hours | Serves: 6**

1 (13 to 14-ounce) can light coconut milk
¼ cup water
2 tablespoons Thai red curry paste
1 pound small red potatoes, quartered
1 small red onion, very thinly sliced
2 tablespoons curry powder
2 teaspoons light brown sugar
½ teaspoon kosher salt
1½ to 2 pounds pork tenderloin
Freshly ground black pepper
Bean sprouts, for serving
Chopped fresh cilantro or basil, for serving

1. In a slow cooker, whisk the coconut milk, water, and curry paste. Stir in the potatoes and onion. 2. Rub the curry powder, brown sugar, and salt all over the pork tenderloin. Nestle the pork into the vegetables. Add a few grinds of black pepper. 3. Cover the slow cooker and cook on low temp setting for 7 hours, until the pork is tender and the flavors have melded. 4. Transfer the pork to a cutting board and slice thinly. 5. Spoon the potatoes, onion, and sauce into wide serving bowls, then top with pork. Garnish with bean sprouts and cilantro.
**Per Serving:** Calories 139; Fat 3.2g; Sodium 45mg; Carbs 26g; Fiber 4g; Sugar 8g; Protein 3g

---

## Coffee Pork Tacos

**Prep time: 15 minutes | Cook time: 9 hours | Serves: 8**

2 tablespoons espresso powder or finely ground coffee
2 teaspoons smoked paprika
2 teaspoons light brown sugar
1 teaspoon kosher salt
1¼ teaspoons garlic powder
¾ teaspoon freshly ground black pepper
1 (3 to 4-pound) boneless pork butt, trimmed of external fat
½ cup freshly squeezed orange juice
16 (6-inch) corn tortillas, warmed just before serving
Shredded cabbage, for serving
Shredded Monterey Jack, pepper Jack, or cheddar cheese, for serving
Guacamole, for serving
Lime wedges, for serving

1. In a bowl, combine the espresso powder, paprika, brown sugar, salt, garlic powder, and pepper. 2. Rub the coffee mixture all over the pork, covering all sides. Place pork in slow cooker and pour the orange juice over the top. 3. Cover the slow cooker and cook on low temp setting for 8 to 9 hours, until the pork is tender and easy to shred. 4. Use forks to shred the pork and serve it in the tortillas topped with cabbage, cheese, guacamole, and lime wedges for squeezing.
**Per Serving:** Calories 409; Fat 18.9g; Sodium 214mg; Carbs 10g; Fiber 1g; Sugar 9g; Protein 48g

## Tangy Teriyaki Beef

**Prep time: 5 minutes | Cook time: 8 hours | Serves: 8**

⅓ cup low-sodium gluten-free tamari or soy sauce
¼ cup no-salt-added chicken stock
¼ cup dry sherry
1 tablespoon minced fresh ginger
1 tablespoon minced garlic
2 pounds cubed beef round or stew beef
Sliced scallions, green and white parts, for garnish
Sesame seeds, for garnish

1. In a slow cooker, whisk the tamari, stock, sherry, ginger, and garlic. Add the beef in a single layer, if possible. 2. Cover the slow cooker and cook on low temp setting for 8 hours, until the beef is tender and cooked through. 3. Using a slotted spoon, transfer the beef to serving plates and drizzle with some of the juices, if desired. 4. Garnish with scallions and sesame seeds and serve immediately.
**Per Serving:** Calories 716; Fat 62.6g; Sodium 302mg; Carbs 18g; Fiber 8g; Sugar 2g; Protein 34g

---

## Healthy Salsa Verde Pork

**Prep time: 15 minutes | Cook time: 8-10 hours | Serves: 4**

**For the Pork**
1 (2-pound) pork tenderloin
1 small onion, sliced

**For the Salsa Verde**
½ pound tomatillos, husks removed
½ jalapeño, seeded and roughly chopped
½ onion, roughly chopped
1 garlic clove, peeled
2 tablespoons chopped fresh cilantro
1 tablespoon freshly squeezed lime juice
¼ teaspoon extra-virgin olive oil
½ teaspoon salt

1. Put the pork loin and onion in the slow cooker. Combine all the salsa ingredients in a food processor and pulse until the desired consistency is achieved. 2. Pour the salsa on top of the pork. Cover the slow cooker and cook on low temp setting for 8 to 10 hours.
**Per Serving:** Calories 427; Fat 18.3g; Sodium 603mg; Carbs 44g; Fiber 6g; Sugar 3g; Protein 23g

# Sweet Pork Tenderloin with Pomegranate Seeds

**Prep time: 15 minutes | Cook time: 8-10 hours | Serves: 6**

**For the Pork**

1½ pounds red potatoes, quartered

1 small red onion, sliced

1 (3-pound) pork tenderloin

**For the Sauce**

¼ cup water

¼ cup apple cider vinegar

¼ cup honey

1 tablespoon ground cinnamon

¼ teaspoon salt

⅛ teaspoon freshly ground black pepper

⅓ cup pomegranate seeds

1. Combine the potatoes and onion in the slow cooker. Place the pork tenderloin on top. 2. In a bowl, whisk all the sauce ingredients. Pour the sauce over the tenderloin. Top with the pomegranate seeds. 3. Cover the slow cooker and cook on low temp setting for 8 to 10 hours.

**Per Serving:** Calories 162; Fat 5.3g; Sodium 1006mg; Carbs 3g; Fiber 2g; Sugar 0g; Protein 25g

# Chapter 5 Fish and Seafood

## Trout with Carrot Mélange

Prep time: 20 minutes | Cook time: 7-9 hours | Serves: 6

4 large orange carrots, peeled and sliced
3 yellow carrots, peeled and sliced
3 purple carrots, peeled and sliced
2 onions, chopped
4 garlic cloves, minced
½ cup Roasted Vegetable Broth
1 teaspoon dried marjoram leaves
1 bay leaf
½ teaspoon salt
6 (5-ounce) trout fillets

1. In a slow cooker, mix the carrots, onions, garlic, vegetable broth, marjoram, bay leaf, and salt. Cover the slow cooker and cook on low temp setting for 7 to 9 hours, or until the carrots are tender. 2. Remove and discard the bay leaf. Add the trout fillets to the slow cooker. 3. Cover the slow cooker and cook on low temp setting for 20 to 30 minutes, or until the fish flakes when tested with a fork.
**Per Serving:** Calories 308; Fat 10.2g; Sodium 456mg; Carbs 23.5g; Fiber 1.5g; Sugar 3.3g; Protein 27.3g

## Shrimp and Scallop Tacos

Prep time: 15 minutes | Cook time: 5 hours 20 minutes | Serves: 4

2 cups Savory Vegetable Broth
2 cups canned white hominy, drained and rinsed
2 medium yellow onions, diced
1 or 2 poblano chiles cored and diced
3 tablespoons ground cumin
1 tablespoon minced garlic
4 teaspoons dried oregano
1½ pounds frozen deveined peeled shrimp, thawed
1½ pounds frozen scallops, thawed
½ teaspoon sea salt
8 to 10 corn tortillas
Shredded cabbage, sliced radishes, chopped fresh cilantro, lime juice, or extra-virgin olive oil, for topping

1. In a slow cooker, combine the broth, hominy, onions, chiles, cumin, garlic, and oregano. 2. Cover the slow cooker and cook on low temp setting for 5 hours, until the vegetables are soft. 3. Remove the lid and add the shrimp and scallops. Replace the lid and cook for an additional 15 to 20 minutes, until the shrimp are pink and the scallops are opaque. 4. Stir in the salt. Spoon about ¼ cup of the cooked posole into a corn tortilla for each serving. 5. Top with shredded cabbage, sliced radishes, chopped cilantro, lime juice, or olive oil. Serve the tacos warm.
**Per Serving:** Calories 238; Fat 10.3g; Sodium 268mg; Carbs 10.3g; Fiber 0.3g; Sugar 9.2g; Protein 23.6g

## Cheesy Salmon with Root Vegetables

**Prep time: 20 minutes | Cook time: 7½-9½ hours | Serves: 6**

4 large carrots, sliced
2 sweet potatoes, peeled and cubed
4 Yukon Gold potatoes, cubed
2 onions, chopped
3 garlic cloves, minced
⅓ cup Roasted Vegetable Broth
1 teaspoon dried thyme leaves
½ teaspoon salt
6 (5-ounce) salmon fillets
⅓ cup grated Parmesan cheese

1. In a slow cooker, mix carrots, sweet potatoes, Yukon Gold potatoes, onions, garlic, vegetable broth, thyme, and salt. 2. Cover the slow cooker and cook on low temp setting for 7 to 9 hours, or until the vegetables are tender. 3. Add the salmon fillets and sprinkle each with some of the cheese. 4. Cover the slow cooker and cook on low temp setting for 30 to 40 minutes, or until the salmon flakes when tested with a fork.
**Per Serving:** Calories 397; Fat 5.5g; Sodium 256mg; Carbs 55.5g; Fiber 2g; Sugar 0.7g; Protein 24.8g

---

## Cheesy Cod with White Potatoes

**Prep time: 15 minutes | Cook time: 6 hours | Serves: 6-8**

Nonstick cooking spray, for greasing
4 tablespoons (½ stick) butter
¼ cup whole-wheat flour
2½ cups 2 percent milk
2 teaspoons garlic powder
½ teaspoon sea salt
½ teaspoon ground black pepper
1½ cups shredded sharp Cheddar cheese
1½ cups grated Parmesan cheese, divided
2 pounds white potatoes, peeled and cut into ½-inch-thick slices
1 pound wild-caught cod (3 or 4 large fillets)
1 lemon
1 teaspoon chopped fresh thyme, plus more for topping
1 teaspoon dried rosemary, plus more for topping

1. Grease the bottom and sides of a slow cooker with cooking spray. 2. Add the butter and melt on high. Add the flour and milk. Whisk for 3 to 4 minutes, until simmering and thickened. 3. Mix in the garlic powder, salt, and black pepper. Whisk in the Cheddar cheese and ¼ cup of Parmesan cheese. 4. Leaving the cheese sauce in the slow cooker, transfer the sauce to a bowl. 5. In the slow cooker, arrange a layer of potatoes on top of the cheese sauce, followed by one-quarter of the cheese sauce from the bowl and a thin sprinkling of Parmesan cheese. 6. Repeat with the potatoes, cheese sauce, and Parmesan cheese (making sure Parmesan is the last layer at the end). Cover the slow cooker and cook on low temp setting for 5 hours, until the potatoes are tender. 7. Remove the lid and arrange the cod in a single layer on top of the potato and cheese layers. 8. Squeeze the lemon lightly over the top of the cod, and top with the thyme and rosemary. Replace the lid and cook for an additional 30 minutes to 1 hour, until the cod has cooked through. 9. Garnish with additional lemon juice, thyme, and rosemary. Serve the gratin warm.
**Per Serving:** Calories 311; Fat 16.3g; Sodium 257mg; Carbs 8.3g; Fiber 0.6g; Sugar 0.7g; Protein 31.3g

## Fish and Vegetable Risotto

**Prep time: 20 minutes | Cook time: 4 hours 45minutes | Serves: 6**

8-ounces cremini mushrooms, sliced
2 onions, chopped
5 garlic cloves, minced
2 cups short-grain brown rice
1 teaspoon dried thyme leaves
6 cups roasted vegetable broth
6 (5-ounce) tilapia fillets
2 cups baby spinach leaves
2 tablespoons unsalted butter
½ cup grated Parmesan cheese

1. In a slow cooker, mix the mushrooms, onions, garlic, rice, thyme, and vegetable broth. Cover the slow cooker and cook on low temp setting for 3 to 4 hours, or until the rice is tender. 2. Put the fish on top of the rice. Cover the slow cooker and cook for 25 to 35 minutes longer, or until the fish flakes when tested with a fork. 3. Gently stir the fish into the risotto. Add the baby spinach leaves. 4. Stir in the butter and cheese. Cover and let cook on low temp setting for 10 minutes, then serve.
**Per Serving:** Calories 358; Fat 9.8g; Sodium 561mg; Carbs 31.5g; Fiber 5g; Sugar 3.7g; Protein 29.1g

## Lemony Salmon with Zucchini and Carrot

**Prep time: 10 minutes | Cook time: 2 hours | Serves: 4**

1 cup no-salt-added vegetable broth or water
½ cup dry white wine
1 (2-pound) salmon fillet, skin on
1 medium lemon, thinly sliced and seeded
1 medium zucchini, shredded
1 large carrot, shredded
3 or 4 (3-inch) thyme sprigs, plus more for garnish
Kosher salt
Freshly ground black pepper

1. Into a slow cooker, pour the broth and wine. Place the salmon, skin-side down, in the slow cooker. 2. Layer the lemon slices on top of the salmon. Evenly distribute the zucchini and carrot on top of the lemon. Add the thyme and spiced with salt and pepper. 3. Cover the slow cooker and cook on low temp setting for 2 hours, until the salmon flakes easily with a fork or reaches an internal temperature of 145°F. 4. Discard the lemon and thyme and serve the salmon with the zucchini and carrots on top. Garnish with fresh thyme leaves.
**Per Serving:** Calories 168; Fat 8.9g; Sodium 269mg; Carbs 2.2g; Fiber 0.2g; Sugar 0.7g; Protein 18.2g

## Spicy Monkfish with Sweet Potatoes

**Prep time: 10 minutes | Cook time: 6 hours | Serves: 6**

Nonstick cooking spray, for greasing
1 cup no-salt-added vegetable broth or chicken stock
1 teaspoon ground cumin
2 medium sweet potatoes, peeled and cut into ½-inch cubes (about 20 ounces)
1 (16-ounce) jar low-sodium salsa verde
1½ pounds monkfish, halibut, cod, or haddock, cut into 2-inch pieces
Sliced green cabbage, for serving
Chopped fresh cilantro, for serving
Plain Greek yogurt, for serving

1. Grease a slow cooker with nonstick spray or brush with oil. In the slow cooker, combine the broth and cumin. Layer in the sweet potatoes, then pour the salsa on top. 2. Cover the slow cooker and cook on low temp setting for 6 hours, until the sweet potatoes are fork-tender. 3. Add the fish to the slow cooker. Cover the slow cooker and cook on high temp setting for 10 to 15 minutes, until the fish flakes easily. 4. Spoon the fish and sweet potatoes into serving bowls and top with the cabbage, cilantro, and yogurt.

**Per Serving:** Calories 194; Fat 4.3g; Sodium 369mg; Carbs 11.2g; Fiber 2.6g; Sugar 2.4g; Protein 22.6g

---

## Shrimp with Corn Chowder

**Prep time: 10 minutes | Cook time: 8 hours | Serves: 6**

¾ pound small red potatoes, quartered
15 ounces frozen corn
⅓ cup whole-wheat flour
1½ teaspoons salt-free Cajun or Creole spicing
6 cups no-salt-added vegetable broth
18 ounces frozen raw shrimp (51/60 count), peeled and deveined
¾ cup half-and-half
Freshly ground black pepper
Thinly sliced scallions, green and white parts, or chopped fresh parsley, for garnish

1. In a slow cooker, combine the potatoes, corn, flour, and Cajun spicing, tossing to evenly distribute the dry ingredients. Pour in the broth. 2. Cover the slow cooker and cook on low temp setting for 7 to 8 hours, until the potatoes are fork-tender. 3. Add the shrimp. Cook on high for 15 to 20 minutes, or until the shrimp are opaque. Stir in the half-and-half and warm through. 4. Spoon into serving bowls, spiced with pepper, and garnish with scallions. Serve immediately.

**Per Serving:** Calories 182; Fat 1.6g; Sodium 258mg; Carbs 1.6g; Fiber 0.3g; Sugar 0.7g; Protein 34.5g

## Pesto Cod with White Bean Ratatouille

**Prep time: 10 minutes | Cook time: 6 hours 30 minutes | Serves: 4**

1 tablespoon extra-virgin olive oil
½ medium sweet or yellow onion, finely chopped
2 tablespoons minced garlic
1 (14-ounce) can no-salt-added diced tomatoes, drained
1-pound eggplant, peeled and cut into 1-inch cubes (about 1 medium eggplant)
2 medium zucchinis, diced
1½ cups no-salt-added cannellini or other white beans, drained and rinsed
2 tablespoons basil pesto, plus 1 teaspoon
4 (4-ounce) cod fillets
Kosher salt
Freshly ground black pepper

1. In a slow cooker, combine the oil, sweet onion, garlic, tomatoes, eggplant, zucchini, beans, and 1 tablespoon of pesto. 2. Cover the slow cooker and cook on low temp setting for 5 to 6 hours, until the eggplant is softened. 3. Brush each cod fillet with 1 teaspoon of pesto. Place the cod on top of the eggplant mixture and cook on low temp setting for 25 to 30 minutes, until the fish flakes easily with a fork. 4. Serve the cod atop the eggplant mixture. Spiced with salt and pepper.
**Per Serving:** Calories 420; Fat 23g; Sodium 369mg; Carbs 31g; Fiber 1g; Sugar 4g; Protein 20g

## Shrimp with Cheesy Grits

**Prep time: 10 minutes | Cook time: 6 hours 20 minutes | Serves: 6**

Nonstick cooking spray, for greasing
2 cups gluten-free stone-ground grits or polenta
6 cups no-salt-added vegetable broth or water
Pinch kosher salt
¼ cup half-and-half
1 cup shredded pepper Jack, Monterey Jack, or cheddar cheese
1 tablespoon unsalted butter or ghee
24 ounces frozen raw shrimp, peeled, deveined, tail-on, and thawed
Freshly ground black pepper
2 teaspoons gluten-free Worcestershire sauce
6 scallions, green and white parts, thinly sliced, for garnish
4 turkey bacon slices, cooked and crumbled, for garnish
Hot sauce, for serving

1. Grease a slow cooker with nonstick spray or brush with oil. In the slow cooker, whisk the grits, vegetable broth, and salt. Cover the slow cooker and cook on low temp setting for 6 hours, until most of the broth is absorbed. 2. Add the half-and-half, pepper Jack cheese, and butter. Stir until the cheese melts. 3. Place the shrimp on top of the grits, spiced with pepper, and drizzle with the Worcestershire sauce. Cover the slow cooker and cook on high temp setting for 15 to 20 minutes, until the shrimp is opaque. 4. Place the shrimp and grits in serving bowls and top with the scallions and bacon. Serve with hot sauce.
**Per Serving:** Calories 180; Fat 13.7g; Sodium 147mg; Carbs 9.6g; Fiber 3g; Sugar 6g; Protein 5.8g

# Cheesy Flounder with Almonds

**Prep time: 15 minutes | Cook time: 2 hours | Serves: 4**

Nonstick spray
4 (4-ounce) fresh or frozen flounder fillets
1 cup (4 ounces) grated Swiss cheese
½ cup slivered almonds
1 tablespoon freeze-dried chives
Sweet paprika, to taste
¼ cup dry white wine
1 tablespoon unsalted butter
½ cup grated carrot
1 tablespoon all-purpose flour
¼ teaspoon dried tarragon
Sea salt, to taste
White pepper, to taste
1 cup evaporated milk

1. Grease slow cooker with nonstick spray. Rinse the fish and pat dry with paper towels. Lay 2 fillets flat in the slow cooker. 2. Sprinkle the grated cheese, almonds, and chives over the fillets. Place the fillets on top. Sprinkle paprika over the fish fillets. Pour the wine around the fish. Add the butter and carrots to a bowl or measuring cup. 3. Cover and microwave on high for 1 minute; stir and microwave on high for 1 more minute. 4. Stir in the flour, tarragon, salt, and pepper. Whisk in the evaporated milk. Cover and microwave on high for 1 minute. Pour the sauce over the fish. 5. Cover the slow cooker and cook on low temp setting for 2 hours or until the fish is cooked through, the cheese is melted, and the sauce is thickened. Let rest for 15 minutes. 6. To serve, use a knife to cut through all layers into four wedges. Spoon each wedge onto a plate. 7. Sprinkle with additional paprika before serving if desired.

**Per Serving:** Calories 221; Fat 4g; Sodium 159mg; Carbs 3g; Fiber 1g; Sugar 2g; Protein 3g

# Chapter 6 Soup, Chili and Stew

## Herbed Split Pea and Carrot Soup

**Prep time: 15 minutes | Cook time: 7-8 hours | Serves: 6**

2 cups dried split peas, soaked in water overnight, drained, and rinsed well
3 carrots, chopped
1 celery stalk, diced
½ medium onion, diced
1 tablespoon extra-virgin olive oil
1 tablespoon freshly squeezed lemon juice
2 teaspoons dried thyme leaves
1 teaspoon garlic powder
½ teaspoon dried oregano
2 bay leaves
8 cups broth of choice

1. In slow cooker, combine the split peas, carrots, celery, onion, olive oil, lemon juice, thyme, garlic powder, oregano, bay leaves, and broth. 2. Cover the slow cooker and set to low temp setting. Cook for 7 to 8 hours. 3. Remove and discard the bay leaves. For a smoother soup, blend with a stick blender and serve.
**Per Serving:** Calories 160; Fat 11.8g; Sodium 255mg; Carbs 9.6g; Fiber 3.9g; Sugar 2g; Protein 7.6g

## Tangy Sweet Potato and Leek Soup

**Prep time: 15 minutes | Cook time: 4-5 hours | Serves: 6**

5 medium sweet potatoes, peeled and chopped
1 leek, washed and sliced
1½ teaspoons garlic powder
1 teaspoon sea salt
½ teaspoon ground turmeric
¼ teaspoon ground cumin
4 cups vegetable broth
Freshly ground black pepper

1. In slow cooker, combine the sweet potatoes, leek, garlic powder, salt, turmeric, cumin, and broth, and spiced with pepper. 2. Cover the slow cooker and set to low temp setting. Cook for 4 to 5 hours. 3. Using a stick blender, purée the soup until smooth and serve.
**Per Serving:** Calories 221; Fat 14g; Sodium 221mg; Carbs 6g; Fiber 4g; Sugar 1g; Protein 11g

## Creamy Wild Rice Stew with Mushrooms

**Prep time: 15 minutes | Cook time: 6-8 hours | Serves: 6**

| | |
|---|---|
| 1½ cups uncooked wild rice | 1 tablespoon extra-virgin olive oil |
| 6 cups vegetable broth | 1 teaspoon sea salt |
| 2 carrots, diced | ½ teaspoon garlic powder |
| 1 celery stalk, diced | ½ teaspoon dried thyme leaves |
| ½ medium onion, diced | 1 bay leaf |
| ¼ cup dried porcini mushrooms | Freshly ground black pepper |

1. In slow cooker, combine the rice, broth, carrots, celery, onion, mushrooms, olive oil, salt, garlic powder, thyme, and bay leaf, and spiced with pepper. 2. Cover the slow cooker and set to low temp setting. Cook for 6 to 8 hours. 3. Remove and discard the bay leaf before serving.

**Per Serving:** Calories 116; Fat 8.4g; Sodium 542mg; Carbs 0.9g; Fiber 0.2g; Sugar 0.1g; Protein 9.1g

## Healthy Butternut Squash Soup

**Prep time: 15 minutes | Cook time: 5-6 hours | Serves: 8**

| | |
|---|---|
| 7 cups diced butternut squash | ½ teaspoon ground cinnamon |
| 1 cup baby carrots | ½ teaspoon sea salt, |
| 1 medium yellow onion, diced | ¼ teaspoon cayenne pepper |
| 1 Granny Smith apple, peeled, cored, and sliced | ⅛ teaspoon ground nutmeg |
| ¼ cup minced garlic | 4 cups savory vegetable broth |
| ½ teaspoon ground black pepper | ¼ cup 2 percent milk, coconut milk, or cashew cream |

1. In a slow cooker, combine the squash, carrots, onion, apple, garlic, black pepper, cinnamon, salt, cayenne, nutmeg, and broth. 2. Cover the slow cooker and cook on low temp setting for 5 to 6 hours, until the squash is soft and easily mashed. 3. Using a stick blender, blend until smooth. Spiced with salt and pepper. 4. Stir in the milk, and serve the soup warm.

**Per Serving:** Calories 200; Fat 5g; Sodium 269mg; Carbs 4g; Fiber 1g; Sugar 1g; Protein 5g

## Delicious BBQ Sauce

**Prep time: 5 minutes | Cook time: 6-8 hours | Serves: 10-12**

- 1 (28-ounce) can tomato puree
- ¾ cup coconut sugar
- 2 teaspoons onion powder
- ¼ cup apple cider vinegar
- ¼ cup honey
- 2 teaspoons whiskey
- 1 tablespoon chili powder
- 1 tablespoon yellow mustard
- 2 teaspoons liquid smoke
- ¼ teaspoon garlic powder
- 1 teaspoon sea salt
- 1 teaspoon ground black pepper

1. In a slow cooker, combine the tomato puree, sugar, onion powder, vinegar, honey, whiskey, chili powder, mustard, liquid smoke, garlic powder, salt, and black pepper. 2. Cover the slow cooker and cook on low temp setting for 6 to 8 hours, until the sauce has thickened. 3. Spoon the sauce into glass containers to store. Let cool to room temperature before refrigerating.

**Per Serving:** Calories 374; Fat 31.7g; Sodium 287mg; Carbs 7g; Fiber 3g; Sugar 1g; Protein 18.7g

## Protein Soup

**Prep time: 15 minutes | Cook time: 5-6 hours | Serves: 6-8**

- 1 tablespoon extra-virgin olive oil
- 5 cups chopped cooked sausage
- 1 (12-ounce) package turkey bacon, chopped
- 2½ cups canned diced and peeled white potatoes, drained
- 1 (15-ounce) can diced tomatoes, drained
- 4 cups savory chicken broth or store-bought chicken broth
- 2 teaspoons minced garlic
- 1 (1-ounce) packet Hollandaise sauce mix
- 6 to 16 scrambled eggs or egg whites

1. In a slow cooker, mix the olive oil, sausage, bacon, potatoes, and tomatoes. 2. In a bowl, combine the broth, garlic, and Hollandaise sauce mix. Mix well. 3. Pour the broth mixture into the slow cooker and stir. Cover the slow cooker and cook on low temp setting for 5 to 6 hours or on high for 4 hours. 4. Serve the soup warm, topped with 1 or 2 scrambled eggs or egg whites per serving.

**Per Serving:** Calories 222; Fat 11g; Sodium 314mg; Carbs 6g; Fiber 4g; Sugar 1g; Protein 12g

## Peppercorn Chicken Stock

**Prep time: 150 minutes | Cook time: 7-10 hours | Serves: 14**

- 6 bone-in, skinless chicken thighs
- 2 celery stalks, cut into 2-inch pieces
- 2 large carrots, cut into 2-inch chunks
- 1 onion, cut into 6 wedges
- 12 cups water
- 1 teaspoon peppercorns
- ½ teaspoon salt
- 1 bay leaf

1. In a slow cooker, mix all the ingredients. Cover the slow cooker and cook on low temp setting for 7 to 10 hours. 2. Remove the solids using tongs and discard. Strain the stock through cheesecloth into a bowl.

**Per Serving:** Calories 191; Fat 6g; Sodium 298mg; Carbs 1.4g; Fiber 0.3g; Sugar 0.1g; Protein 31.2g

## Herbed Chicken Barley Stew

**Prep time: 20 minutes | Cook time: 8-10 hours | Serves: 8**

- 2 onions, chopped
- 4 garlic cloves, minced
- 4 large carrots, sliced
- 1¼ cups hulled barley
- 10 boneless, skinless chicken thighs, cut into 2-inch pieces
- 1½ cups frozen corn
- 8 cups chicken stock
- 1 sprig fresh rosemary
- 1 teaspoon dried thyme leaves
- 2 cups baby spinach leaves

1. In a slow cooker, mix the onions, garlic, carrots, and barley. Top with the chicken and corn. 2. Pour the chicken stock over all and add the rosemary and thyme leaves. 3. Cover the slow cooker and cook on low temp setting for 8 to 10 hours, or until the chicken and the barley is tender. 4. Stir in the spinach leaves. Cover and let stand for 5 minutes, then serve.

**Per Serving:** Calories 270; Fat 15g; Sodium 411mg; Carbs 5g; Fiber 3g; Sugar 2g; Protein 9g

## Garlicky Fish Stock

**Prep time: 15 minutes | Cook time: 4-6 hours | Serves: 12**

2 pounds shrimp shells, fish bones, and crab shells
½ cup chopped leek
11 cups water
1 tablespoon freshly squeezed lemon juice
1 onion, cut into 4 wedges
5 garlic cloves, peeled and smashed
½ teaspoon white peppercorns
½ teaspoon salt
1 (14-ounce) BPA-free can diced tomatoes, undrained
½ teaspoon dried thyme leaves

1. In a slow cooker, mix all the ingredients. 2. Cover the slow cooker and cook on low temp setting for 4 to 6 hours. Do not cook this stock recipe longer, or it may become bitter. 3. Remove the solids using tongs and discard. Strain the stock through cheesecloth into a bowl.
**Per Serving:** Calories 93; Fat 6.6g; Sodium 277mg; Carbs 1g; Fiber 0.2g; Sugar 0g; Protein 7.7g

## Wild Rice with Vegetable Soup

**Prep time: 20 minutes | Cook time: 7-9 hours | Serves: 8**

1½ cups wild rice, rinsed and drained
2 onions, chopped
1 leek, chopped
5 garlic cloves, sliced
2 cups sliced cremini mushrooms
4 carrots, peeled and sliced
2 cups frozen corn
8 cups Roasted Vegetable Broth
1 teaspoon dried thyme leaves
2 cups chopped kale

1. In a slow cooker, mix the wild rice, onions, leek, garlic, mushrooms, carrots, and corn. 2. Pour the vegetable broth overall and add the thyme leaves. 3. Cover the slow cooker and cook on low temp setting for 7 to 9 hours, or until the vegetables and wild rice are tender. 4. Stir in the kale. Cover the slow cooker and cook on low temp setting for another 20 minutes, or until the kale wilts.
**Per Serving:** Calories 216; Fat 11g; Sodium 230mg; Carbs 5g; Fiber 3g; Sugar 1g; Protein 9g

## Chickpea and Carrots Soup

**Prep time: 20 minutes | Cook time: 5-6 hours | Serves: 8**

- 2 onions, chopped
- 3 garlic cloves, minced
- 4 carrots, peeled and cut into chunks
- 2 medium parsley roots, peeled and sliced
- 2 (14-ounce) cans diced tomatoes, undrained
- 2 (15-ounce) cans no-salt-added chickpeas, drained and rinsed
- 6 cups Roasted Vegetable Broth
- 1 teaspoon dried basil leaves
- ¼ teaspoon freshly ground black pepper

1. In a slow cooker, layer all of the ingredients. Cover the slow cooker and cook on low temp setting for 5 to 6 hours, or until the vegetables are tender. 2. Stir the soup and serve topped with pesto, if desired.
**Per Serving:** Calories 230; Fat 15.9g; Sodium 300mg; Carbs 15.9g; Fiber 9.3g; Sugar 3g; Protein 10g

## Delicious Bone Broth

**Prep time: 15 minutes | Cook time: 8-10 hours | Serves: 16**

- 4 pounds beef bones
- 4 carrots, chopped
- 3 celery stalks, chopped
- 2 onions, chopped
- 6 garlic cloves, smashed
- 1 teaspoon black peppercorns
- 1 bay leaf
- 2 tablespoons freshly squeezed lemon juice
- 1 teaspoon salt
- 14 cups water

1. In a large roasting pan, roast the bones at 400°F for about 20 to 25 minutes, or until browned. 2. In a slow cooker, add the bones and the ingredients. 3. Cover the slow cooker and cook on low temp setting for 8 to 10 hours, or until the broth is a deep brown. 4. Remove the solids using tongs and discard. Strain the broth through cheesecloth into a very bowl.
**Per Serving:** Calories 271; Fat 14g; Sodium 288mg; Carbs 5g; Fiber 3g; Sugar 5g; Protein 11g

## Creamy Zucchini Soup

**Prep time: 5 minutes | Cook time: 8 hours | Serves: 4**

3 zucchinis, cut in chunks
4 cups vegetable broth
2 tablespoons low fat sour cream

2 cloves garlic, minced
Spicing: salt, pepper, thyme, basil to taste

1. Combine all ingredients except sour cream in a slow cooker Close the lid. Cook for 6-8 hours on low temp setting. 2. Add sour cream and using a blender make a smooth purée. Serve hot with Parmesan cheese if desired.
**Per Serving:** Calories 142; Fat 10.2g; Sodium 269mg; Carbs 4.9g; Fiber 2.7g; Sugar 2g; Protein 8.8g

## Beef & Butternut Squash Stew

**Prep time: 20 minutes | Cook time: 8 hours | Serves: 5-6**

2 lb. beef stew meat
½ lb. bacon, diced
2 cups butternut squash, diced
1 cup button mushrooms
½ yellow onion, minced
3 garlic cloves, minced
½ teaspoon garlic powder

½ teaspoon salt
8-10 sage leaves, minced
bouquet of herbs (rosemary, thyme, and sage) tied in a cheesecloth bag.
1 qt beef bone broth
½ cup red wine

1. In a sauté pan cook the bacon until crispy over medium heat. Add the meat to the hot pan with the bacon grease, and sprinkle with garlic powder and salt. Brown on all sides for about 8 minutes. Set aside. 2. Add sage, onion and garlic to the pan and let sweat until the onions are translucent. 3. Add the mixture to a slow cooker along with all the other ingredients and mix to combine. Cover the slow cooker and cook for 8 hours on low.
**Per Serving:** Calories 220; Fat 13g; Sodium 321mg; Carbs 6g; Fiber 4g; Sugar 2g; Protein 12g

## Turkey & Spinach Soup

**Prep time: 5 minutes | Cook time: 6 hours | Serves: 4**

6 cups turkey stock
2 cups boiled turkey meat, cubed
4 cups fresh spinach, chopped
1 tablespoon ginger and garlic mixture, half of each
Salt, pepper to taste

1. Put all the ingredients into the slow cooker. Close the lid and cook for 6 hours on low. 2. When done you can either serve it as is or use a blender to make a puréed soup. Serve hot with toast.
**Per Serving:** Calories 175; Fat 8g; Sodium 326mg; Carbs 5g; Fiber 0.2g; Sugar 0.3g; Protein 1g


## Spicy Chicken Tortilla Soup

**Prep time: 15 minutes | Cook time: 6 hours | Serves: 8**

1 small yellow onion, finely chopped
4 garlic cloves, minced
1 small jalapeño pepper, seeded and finely chopped
2 teaspoons ground cumin
1 tablespoon chili powder
1 (14½-ounce) can no-salt-added fire-roasted tomatoes or diced tomatoes, with their juices
1 (15- to 16-ounce) can no-salt-added black beans, drained and rinsed
1 cup frozen corn
1 pound boneless, skinless chicken breasts
4 cups no-salt-added chicken stock or vegetable broth
8 ounces gluten-free tricolor tortilla strips or baked tortilla chips, for serving
Chopped fresh cilantro, for serving
Lime wedges, for serving

1. In a slow cooker, combine the onion, garlic, jalapeño, cumin, chili powder, tomatoes with their juices, beans, and corn. Nestle in the chicken breasts and add the chicken stock. 2. Cover the slow cooker and cook on low temp setting for 5 to 6 hours, until the chicken is cooked through and falling apart. 3. Using 2 forks, shred the chicken in the pot. Stir to distribute. Spoon into serving bowls and top with the tortilla strips and cilantro. 4. Serve with lime wedges.
**Per Serving:** Calories 221; Fat 9.4g; Sodium 321mg; Carbs 8.6g; Fiber 2g; Sugar 1g; Protein 14.2g

## Creamy Cauliflower Soup

**Prep time: 5 minutes | Cook time: 4 hours 15 minutes | Serves: 4**

1 cauliflower head, stalk removed, chopped
4-5 cups chicken broth
1 cup leeks, diced
½ cup cream
Salt, pepper to taste

1. Pour the broth into a slow cooker, add chopped cauliflower and diced leeks, spiced with salt and pepper. 2. Close the lid and cook for 4 hours on low. Open the lid and add the cream, cook with the lid open for 15 minutes more. 3. Using a hand blender purée the soup and serve hot.
**Per Serving:** Calories 226; Fat 9.3g; Sodium 324mg; Carbs 8.7g; Fiber 3g; Sugar 2g; Protein 12.6g

## Lemon Chickpea Soup

**Prep time: 15 minutes | Cook time: 6 hours | Serves: 6**

1 tablespoon extra-virgin olive oil
1½ cups no-salt-added chickpeas, drained and rinsed
6 cups no-salt-added vegetable broth or chicken stock
1 medium yellow onion, finely chopped
3 medium carrots, thinly sliced
2 celery ribs, thinly sliced
1 tablespoon minced garlic
3 (4-inch) thyme sprigs or ½ teaspoon dried thyme leaves
Freshly ground black pepper
¼ teaspoon kosher salt
1 bay leaf
1 lemon, cut into 6 wedges, for serving

1. In a slow cooker, combine the oil, chickpeas, vegetable broth, onion, carrots, celery, garlic, thyme, pepper, salt, and bay leaf. 2. Cover the slow cooker and cook on low temp setting for 6 hours, until the vegetables have softened. Remove and discard the bay leaf. 3. Spoon into serving bowls and add a squeeze of juice from 1 lemon wedge to each serving.
**Per Serving:** Calories 228; Fat 11.2g; Sodium 541mg; Carbs 10.3g; Fiber 4g; Sugar 2g; Protein 13.2g

# Italian Chicken with Spaghetti Soup

**Prep time: 10 minutes | Cook time: 6 hours | Serves: 6**

1 (14½-ounce) can no-salt-added petite diced tomatoes, with their juices
1 medium yellow onion, finely chopped
1 tablespoon minced garlic
1 large green bell pepper, finely chopped
4 cups no-salt-added chicken stock or vegetable broth
1 tablespoon Italian spicing
¼ teaspoon freshly ground black pepper, plus more for spicing
1 bay leaf
12 ounces boneless, skinless chicken breast
Kosher salt
2 ounces whole-grain thin spaghetti noodles, broken into 2-inch lengths
Chopped fresh basil, for garnish

1. In a slow cooker, combine the tomatoes with their juices, the onion, garlic, bell pepper, chicken stock, Italian spicing, black pepper, and bay leaf. 2. Spiced the chicken on both sides with salt and additional black pepper, then add it to the pot, nestling it into the tomato mixture. 3. Cover the slow cooker and cook on low temp setting for 5 to 6 hours, until the chicken is no longer pink inside and shreds easily. 4. Remove the chicken and bay leaf from the slow cooker. Discard the bay leaf. Stir in the noodles and cook, covered, on high for 15 to 20 minutes, until the noodles are tender. 5. While the noodles are cooking, use 2 forks to shred the chicken. Return the chicken to the slow cooker and stir. Spiced with salt and pepper. 6. Spoon the soup into bowls, garnish with basil, and serve.

**Per Serving:** Calories 224; Fat 12.3g; Sodium 458mg; Carbs 11.2g; Fiber 2g; Sugar 1g; Protein 14.2g

# Chapter 7 Sauce, Dip and Dressings

## Buffalo Cashews Dip

Prep time: 15 minutes | Cook time: 5-6 hours | Serves: 6

1-pound cauliflower, chopped
1¼ cups raw cashews, soaked in water overnight, drained
¾ cup hot sauce
½ cup water
1 tablespoon freshly squeezed lemon juice
1 teaspoon garlic powder
½ teaspoon paprika
Sea salt
Freshly ground black pepper
Chopped veggies, for serving

1. In slow cooker, combine the cauliflower, cashews, hot sauce, water, lemon juice, garlic powder, and paprika. Spiced with salt and pepper. 2. Cover the slow cooker and set to low temp setting. Cook for 5 to 6 hours. 3. Transfer the mixture to a blender or food processor. Pulse until the desired consistency is reached. Serve with chopped veggies.
**Per Serving:** Calories 263; Fat 9.2g; Sodium 211mg; Carbs 8.6g; Fiber 2g; Sugar 1g; Protein 8.7g

## Avocado Sauce

Prep time: 10 minutes | Cook time: 0 minutes | Serves: 10

1 large, ripe avocado, peeled and pitted
2 teaspoons fresh dill
2 teaspoons freshly squeezed lemon juice
½ teaspoon sea salt
Dash red pepper flakes
Chopped veggies, for serving (if desired)

1. In a blender, combine the avocado, dill, lemon juice, salt, and red pepper flakes. Pulse until smooth. 2. If the sauce is too thick, add water to thin as needed. Serve with chopped veggies.
**Per Serving:** Calories 187; Fat 12.4g; Sodium 110mg; Carbs 8.9g; Fiber 2g; Sugar 1g; Protein 4.7g

## Classical Marinara Sauce

**Prep time: 20 minutes | Cook time: 6-8 hours | Serves: 12**

4 pounds Roma tomatoes, chopped
4 beefsteak tomatoes, seeded and chopped
1 (6-ounce) can tomato paste
2 onions, peeled and chopped
4 garlic cloves, peeled and minced
½ cup shredded carrot
1 bay leaf
2 teaspoons dried basil leaves
1 teaspoon dried oregano leaves

1. In a slow cooker, mix all the ingredients. Cover the slow cooker and cook on low temp setting for 6 to 8 hours. 2. Remove and discard the bay leaf. 3. Divide the sauce into 2-cup portions and freeze up to 4 months.
**Per Serving:** Calories 79; Fat 2g; Sodium 332mg; Carbs 12g; Fiber 2g; Sugar 4g; Protein 4g

---

## Saucy Bolognese Sauce

**Prep time: 20 minutes | Cook time: 7-9 hours | Serves: 12**

2 pounds lean grass-fed ground beef
2 onions, chopped
7 garlic cloves, minced
1 large carrot, grated
¼ cup tomato paste
3 pounds Roma tomatoes, seeded and chopped
2 cups bottled tomato juice
1 bay leaf
1 teaspoon dried oregano leaves
½ teaspoon salt

1. In a large skillet, mix the ground beef, onions, and garlic. Cook over medium heat, stirring frequently to break up the meat, until the beef is browned. Drain. 2. In a slow cooker, mix the beef mixture with the ingredients. 3. Cover the slow cooker and cook on low temp setting for 7 to 9 hours, or until the sauce is thickened.
**Per Serving:** Calories 85; Fat 2.9g; Sodium 233mg; Carbs 9g; Fiber 4g; Sugar 2g; Protein 2.7g

## Tomato Sauce

**Prep time: 20 minutes | Cook time: 9-11 hours | Serves: 13**

4 pounds Roma tomatoes, seeded and chopped
2 onions, chopped
5 garlic cloves, minced
3 tablespoons extra-virgin olive oil
2 cups bottled tomato juice
3 tablespoons tomato paste
2 teaspoons dried basil leaves
½ teaspoon salt
⅛ teaspoon white pepper

1. In a slow cooker, place all the tomatoes. Partially cover the slow cooker and cook the tomatoes on high for 3 hours, stirring the tomatoes twice during cooking time. 2. Add the ingredients. 3. Cover the slow cooker and cook on low temp setting for 6 to 8 hours longer, until the sauce is bubbling and the consistency you want.
**Per Serving:** Calories 263; Fat 6g; Sodium 200mg; Carbs 28.3g; Fiber 11g; Sugar 10g; Protein 13g

---

## Cheesy Artichoke and Spinach Sauce

**Prep time: 10 minutes | Cook time: 2-4 hours | Serves: 4**

1 9 oz. box of frozen spinach, thawed and squeezed to drain
1 (14 oz.) can quartered artichoke hearts, drained and chopped
½ cup Alfredo sauce
½ cup mayonnaise
¾ teaspoon garlic salt
¼ teaspoon pepper
1 cup shredded Swiss cheese

1. Mix all ingredients in a large slow cooker. 2. Cover the slow cooker and cook on low temp setting for 2 to 4 hours before serving. 3. Serve with crackers or toasted bread.
**Per Serving:** Calories 195; Fat 18.3g; Sodium 278mg; Carbs 5.4g; Fiber 1g; Sugar 2g; Protein 5.8g

## Cheesy Buffalo Chicken Dip

Prep time: 10 minutes | Cook time: 30 minutes | Serves: 4

3 (10 oz.) cans of chicken (drained)
2 (8 oz.) packages of cream cheese (softened)
8 oz. buffalo wing sauce
6 oz. ranch or blue cheese dressing
2 cups Cheddar cheese

1. Preheat a slow cooker to 350°F. 2. In a bowl, mix all the ingredients with the shredded chicken. 3. Put the dip mixture into a casserole dish and bake for 30 minutes.

**Per Serving:** Calories 382; Fat 0.6g; Sodium 711mg; Carbs 62.6g; Fiber 12g; Sugar 14g; Protein 62.5g

## Spiced Smoky Barbecue Sauce

Prep time: 10 minutes | Cook time: 6-8 hours | Serves: 6

2 cups tomato purée
1 small sweet onion, finely chopped
3 garlic cloves, minced
¾ cup apple cider vinegar
½ cup molasses or maple syrup
1 tablespoon mustard
1 tablespoon chili powder
2 tablespoons gluten-free vegetarian Worcestershire sauce
2 teaspoons liquid smoke
½ teaspoon white pepper
¼ teaspoon kosher salt

1. In a slow cooker, stir the tomato purée, onion, garlic, vinegar, molasses, mustard, chili powder, Worcestershire sauce, liquid smoke, pepper, and salt. 2. Cook on low temp setting for 6 to 8 hours, until the sauce is thick.

**Per Serving:** Calories 26; Fat 0.6g; Sodium 123mg; Carbs 3.4g; Fiber 0g; Sugar 0g; Protein 1.4g

## Tangy Cinnamon-Berry Sauce

**Prep time: 5 minutes | Cook time: 2 hours 30 minutes | Serves: 2**

| | |
|---|---|
| 1 (12-ounce) bag fresh or frozen cranberries | ½ cup water |
| 6 ounces fresh or frozen raspberries | 1 (3-inch) cinnamon stick |
| ½ cup maple syrup or honey | Grated zest from 1 medium orange |

1. In a slow cooker, combine the cranberries, raspberries, maple syrup, water, and cinnamon stick. 2. Cover the slow cooker and cook on high temp setting for 2 hours, until the cranberries have all popped open. If they haven't, stir well and cook for another 30 minutes on high. 3. Remove the cinnamon stick and stir in the orange zest. Let the sauce cool to room temperature.

**Per Serving:** Calories 273; Fat 23g; Sodium 111mg; Carbs 8g; Fiber 2g; Sugar 1g; Protein 8g

---

## Herbed Meat Sauce

**Prep time: 10 minutes | Cook time: 8 hours | Serves: 8**

| | |
|---|---|
| 8 ounces lean ground beef | 2 teaspoons dried basil |
| 1-pound ground Italian pork sausage | 1 teaspoon garlic powder |
| 1 (28-ounce) can crushed tomatoes | 1 teaspoon brown sugar |
| 1 (14.5-ounce) can diced tomatoes with green peppers, celery, and onions | ½ teaspoon dried oregano |
| | Salt |
| 2 tablespoons tomato paste | Freshly ground black pepper |
| 1 bay leaf | |

1. Combine the ground beef and ground Italian sausage in the slow cooker. 2. Break up the meat with a wooden spoon. Add the crushed tomatoes, diced tomatoes with their juice, tomato paste, bay leaf, basil, garlic powder, brown sugar, and oregano. Stir well to combine. 3. Cover the slow cooker and cook on low temp setting for 8 hours. 4. Discard the bay leaf and stir. Spiced with salt and pepper and serve.

**Per Serving:** Calories 92; Fat 9g; Sodium 104mg; Carbs 2g; Fiber 0.2g; Sugar 0.1g; Protein 5g

## Easy Rustic Marinara Sauce

**Prep time: 5 minutes | Cook time: 7-8 hours | Serves: 12**

6 pounds Roma tomatoes, chopped
1 (6-ounce) can tomato paste
6 garlic cloves, minced
1 large onion, finely chopped
1 medium red bell pepper, chopped
1 medium carrot, shredded

2 teaspoons dried basil
1 teaspoon dried oregano
½ teaspoon dried thyme
½ teaspoon dried marjoram
½ teaspoon crushed red pepper flakes

1. Combine all the ingredients in a slow cooker. Cover the slow cooker and cook on low temp setting for 7 to 8 hours. 2. If desired, use a stick blender after cooking to crush the tomatoes to desired consistency. 3. Use immediately or freeze in 1- to 2-cup portions in airtight containers for up to 4 months.
**Per Serving:** Calories 95; Fat 6g; Sodium 132mg; Carbs 6g; Fiber 1.8g; Sugar 0.6g; Protein 3g

## Italian-style Bolognese Sauce

**Prep time: 15 minutes | Cook time: 7-8 hours | Serves: 8**

1 tablespoon extra-virgin olive oil
1 pound 93% lean ground beef
1 medium onion, roughly chopped
4 garlic cloves, minced
5 to 6 pounds tomatoes, seeded and chopped
1 medium carrot, roughly chopped
1 dried bay leaf

1 teaspoon dried oregano
1 teaspoon dried basil
¼ cup tomato paste
Freshly ground black pepper
Honey
¼ cup red wine

1. Optional step: In a large skillet, heat the oil over medium-high heat. Add the ground beef, onion, and garlic. 2. Cover the slow cooker and cook. Stirring frequently until beef is browned, 7 to 10 minutes. Drain any excess fat and liquid from the beef. 3. Combine the beef, onion, garlic, tomatoes, carrot, bay leaf, oregano, basil, tomato paste, black pepper, honey, and wine in a slow cooker. Stir to combine. 4. Cover the slow cooker and cook on low temp setting for 7 to 8 hours or until the sauce is thickened.
**Per Serving:** Calories 88; Fat 6g; Sodium 102mg; Carbs 9g; Fiber 2.3g; Sugar 1.2g; Protein 1g

## Creamy Cashews Sauce

**Prep time: 5 minutes | Cook time: 7-8 hours | Serves: 4**

3 cups Savory Vegetable Broth
1 cup raw cashews
1 cup water
½ cup unsweetened soymilk
½ cup nutritional yeast

1 teaspoon dried mustard
2 garlic cloves, minced
Juice of ½ lemon
Pinch salt

1. Combine all the ingredients in a slow cooker and stir well. 2. Cover the slow cooker and cook on low temp setting for 7 to 8 hours, until the cashews are softened. 3. Purée the sauce until smooth using a stick blender. 4. Serve warm.
**Per Serving:** Calories 280; Fat 12g; Sodium 678mg; Carbs 6g; Fiber 4g; Sugar 2g; Protein 14g

# Chapter 8 Desserts and Drinks

## Blueberry-Peach Oats Cobbler

Prep time: 15 minutes | Cook time: 2 hours | Serves: 6

5 tablespoons coconut oil, divided
3 large peaches, peeled and sliced
2 cups frozen blueberries
1 cup almond flour
1 cup rolled oats

1 tablespoon maple syrup
1 tablespoon coconut sugar
1 teaspoon ground cinnamon
½ teaspoon vanilla extract
Pinch ground nutmeg

1. Grease slow cooker with 1 tablespoon of coconut oil. 2. Arrange the peaches and blueberries along the slow cooker. 3. In a bowl, stir the almond flour, oats, 4 tablespoons of coconut oil, maple syrup, coconut sugar, cinnamon, vanilla, and nutmeg until a coarse mixture forms. Gently crumble the topping over the fruit in the slow cooker. 4. Cover the slow cooker and set to high temp setting. Cook for 2 hours and serve.
**Per Serving:** Calories 240; Fat 4.3g; Sodium 278mg; Carbs 47g; Fiber 7g; Sugar 3g; Protein 6g

## Baked Apples with Pecans

Prep time: 15 minutes | Cook time: 2-3 hours | Serves: 5

5 apples
½ cup water
½ cup crushed pecans
¼ cup melted coconut oil

1 teaspoon ground cinnamon
½ teaspoon ground ginger
¼ teaspoon ground cardamom
¼ teaspoon ground cloves

1. Core each apple, and peel off a thin strip from the top of each. 2. Add the water to the slow cooker. Gently place each apple upright along the bottom. 3. In a bowl, stir the pecans, coconut oil, cinnamon, ginger, cardamom, and cloves. Drizzle the mixture over the tops of the apples. 4. Cover the slow cooker and set to high temp setting. Cook for 2 to 3 hours, until the apples soften, and serve.
**Per Serving:** Calories 232; Fat 8.5g; Sodium 465mg; Carbs 38g; Fiber 1g; Sugar 15g; Protein 2g

## Coconut-Cacao Brownies

**Prep time: 15 minutes | Cook time: 2½-3 hours | Serves: 6**

3 tablespoons coconut oil, divided
1 cup almond butter
1 cup unsweetened cacao powder
½ cup coconut sugar
2 large eggs
2 ripe bananas
2 teaspoons vanilla extract
1 teaspoon baking soda
½ teaspoon sea salt

1. Grease the slow cooker with 1 tablespoon of coconut oil. 2. In a bowl, combine the almond butter, cacao powder, coconut sugar, eggs, bananas, vanilla, baking soda, and salt. 3. Mash the bananas and stir well until a batter forms. Pour the batter into the slow cooker. 4. Cover the slow cooker and set to low temp setting. 5. Cook for 2½ to 3 hours, until firm to a light touch but still gooey in the middle, and serve.
**Per Serving:** Calories 567; Fat 16.3g; Sodium 478mg; Carbs 19g; Fiber 14g; Sugar 6g; Protein 18g

---

## Chai Latte

**Prep time: 10 minutes | Cook time: 4 hours | Serves: 8**

8 chai tea bags
2 or 3 decaf black tea bags
8 cups 2 percent milk
3 tablespoons pure maple syrup or liquid stevia
Ground cinnamon, for topping
1 cup light whipped cream, for topping

1. Put the chai tea bags and black tea bags in a slow cooker, then pour in the milk and maple syrup and stir. Cover the slow cooker and cook on low temp setting for 4 hours, until heated through and fragrant. 2. Discard the tea bags. Serve the latte warm in mugs, topped with a sprinkle of ground cinnamon or 2 tablespoons of light whipped cream per serving. Do not use the toppings if you are in the liquids stage. 3. Refrigerate leftovers for up to 1 week, or freeze for up to 1 month.
**Per Serving:** Calories 169; Fat 1.5g; Sodium 629mg; Carbs 36g; Fiber 6g; Sugar 14g; Protein 8g

## Chocolate Chip Lava Cake

**Prep time: 15 minutes | Cook time: 4-5 hours | Serves: 12**

1 tablespoon coconut oil, plus ½ cup
1 (16-ounce) box sugar-free devil's food cake mix, such as Pillsbury
1¼ cups 2 percent milk, plus 2 cups
3 large eggs
1 (4-ounce) box sugar-free instant chocolate pudding mix, such as Jell-O or Royal brands
¾ cup coconut sugar
1 (12-ounce) bag semisweet chocolate chips
2½ to 3 cups no-sugar-added vanilla ice cream
1¼ to 1½ cups light whipped cream, for topping

1. Grease the bottom and sides of a slow cooker with 1 tablespoon of coconut oil. 2. To make the cake batter, in a bowl, beat the cake mix, 1¼ cups of milk, the ½ cup of coconut oil, and the eggs until combined. 3. Pour the cake batter into the slow cooker in an even layer. 4. To make the topping, in a bowl, combine the pudding mix, sugar, and 2 cups of milk. 5. Pour the topping over the cake batter. Do not stir. 6. Sprinkle the chocolate chips over the topping. Cover the slow cooker and cook on low temp setting for 4 to 5 hours, until the top is spongy and the inside is gooey. 7. Serve the cake warm with ¼ cup of ice cream per serving or 2 tablespoons of light whipped cream per serving. 8. Refrigerate leftovers for up to 5 days, or freeze for up to 2 months.
**Per Serving:** Calories 505; Fat 38.1g; Sodium 264mg; Carbs 6g; Fiber 2g; Sugar 3g; Protein 34g

## Stewed Fruit with Herbs

**Prep time: 15 minutes | Cook time: 6-8 hours | Serves: 12**

2 cups dried apricots
2 cups prunes
2 cups dried unsulfured pears
2 cups dried apples
1 cup dried cranberries
¼ cup honey
6 cups water
1 teaspoon dried thyme leaves
teaspoon dried basil leaves

1. In a slow cooker, mix all of the ingredients. 2. Cover the slow cooker and cook on low temp setting for 6 to 8 hours, or until the fruits have absorbed the liquid and are tender.
**Per Serving:** Calories 175; Fat 8g; Sodium 326mg; Carbs 5g; Fiber 0.2g; Sugar 0.3g; Protein 1g

Chapter 8 Desserts and Drinks

## Tangy Apple Cider Wassail

**Prep time: 10 minutes | Cook time: 6-8 hours | Serves: 10**

- 8 cups apple cider
- 2 cups no-sugar-added orange juice
- 1 cup no-sugar-added cranberry juice
- 5 cinnamon sticks
- 10 whole cloves
- ½ teaspoon ground nutmeg
- ½ teaspoon ground ginger
- 1 orange, sliced
- 1 apple, sliced
- ¼ cup cranberries

1. In a slow cooker, mix the apple cider, orange juice, cranberry juice, cinnamon sticks, cloves, nutmeg, and ginger. 2. Cover the slow cooker and cook on low temp setting for 6 to 8 hours, until the mixture is heated through and fragrant. 3. When there are 20 to 30 minutes left of cooking time, remove the lid and add the orange, apple, and cranberries. Replace the lid and cook for another 20 to 30 minutes. 4. Serve the wassail warm in mugs. If you are in the liquids stage, strain and discard the solids before serving. 5. Refrigerate leftovers for up to 1 week, or freeze for up to 1 month.
**Per Serving:** Calories 281; Fat 17.2g; Sodium 407mg; Carbs 4g; Fiber 2g; Sugar 1g; Protein 28g

## Nutty Apple-Peach Crumble

**Prep time: 20 minutes | Cook time: 4-5 hours | Serves: 8**

- 6 large Granny Smith apples, peeled and cut into chunks
- 4 large peaches, peeled and sliced
- 3 tablespoons honey
- 2 tablespoons lemon juice
- 1 cup almond flour
- 1 teaspoon ground cinnamon
- 3 cups quick-cooking oatmeal
- ⅓ cup coconut sugar
- ½ cup slivered almonds
- ½ cup coconut oil, melted

1. In a slow cooker, mix the apples, peaches, honey, and lemon juice. 2. In a bowl, mix the almond flour, cinnamon, oatmeal, coconut sugar, and almonds until well combined. 3. Add the coconut oil and mix until crumbly. 4. Sprinkle the almond mixture over the fruit in the slow cooker. 5. Cover the slow cooker and cook on low temp setting for 4 to 5 hours, or until the fruit is tender and the crumble is bubbling around the edges.
**Per Serving:** Calories 354; Fat 7.9g; Sodium 704mg; Carbs 6g; Fiber 3.6g; Sugar 6g; Protein 18g

## Healthy Berry Oats Crumble

**Prep time: 20 minutes | Cook time: 5-6 hours | Serves: 12**

3 cups frozen organic blueberries
3 cups frozen organic raspberries
3 cups frozen organic strawberries
2 tablespoons lemon juice
2½ cups rolled oats

1 cup whole-wheat flour
⅓ cup maple sugar
1 teaspoon ground cinnamon
⅓ cup coconut oil, melted

1. Do not thaw the berries. In a slow cooker, mix the frozen berries. Drizzle with the lemon juice. 2. In a bowl, mix the oats, flour, maple sugar, and cinnamon until well combined. Stir in the melted coconut oil until crumbly. 3. Sprinkle the oat mixture over the fruit in the slow cooker. 4. Cover the slow cooker and cook on low temp setting for 5 to 6 hours, or until the fruit is bubbling and the topping is browned.
**Per Serving:** Calories 281; Fat 17.2g; Sodium 407mg; Carbs 4g; Fiber 2g; Sugar 1g; Protein 28g

## Peachy Brown Betty with Cranberries

**Prep time: 20 minutes | Cook time: 5-6 hours | Serves: 10**

8 ripe peaches, peeled and cut into chunks
1 cup dried cranberries
2 tablespoons freshly squeezed lemon juice
3 tablespoons honey
3 cups cubed whole-wheat bread

1½ cups whole-wheat bread crumbs
⅓ cup coconut sugar
¼ teaspoon ground cardamom
⅓ cup melted coconut oil

1. In a slow cooker, mix the peaches, dried cranberries, lemon juice, and honey. 2. In a bowl, mix the bread cubes, bread crumbs, coconut sugar, and cardamom. Drizzle the melted coconut oil over all and toss to Grease. 3. Sprinkle the bread mixture on the fruit in the slow cooker. 4. Cover the slow cooker and cook on low temp setting for 5 to 6 hours, or until the fruit is bubbling and the topping is browned.
**Per Serving:** Calories 685; Fat 35g; Sodium 239mg; Carbs 4g; Fiber 2g; Sugar 1g; Protein 26g

## Chocolate-Toffee Lava Cake

**Prep time: 15 minutes | Cook time: 4 hours 45 minutes | Serves: 12**

1 box (4-serving size) chocolate instant pudding & pie filling mix
1 box (4-serving size) butterscotch instant pudding & pie filling mix
1 box dark chocolate cake mix
1 cup sour cream
⅓ cup butter or margarine, melted
3 eggs
3¼ cups milk
1 bag (8 oz.) toffee bits
1 teaspoon vanilla extract
8 oz. frozen whipped topping, thawed

1. Grease a 5-quart oval slow cooker with cooking spray. In a bowl, using an electric mixer beat cake mix, chocolate pudding mix, 1¼ cups of the milk, sour cream, butter, the eggs and vanilla extract. Stir in 1 cup of the toffee bits. Pour batter into the slow cooker. 2. In a 2-quart saucepan, heat 2 cups milk over medium heat for 3 to 5 minutes, stirring frequently, until hot and bubbly. 3. Remove from heat. Sprinkle butterscotch pudding mix over batter in the slow cooker. Slowly pour hot milk over pudding. 4. Cover the slow cooker and cook on low-heat setting 4 hours 30 minutes or until edge of cake is set for at least 2 inches from the side of the slow cooker but center still jiggles slightly when moved. 5. Turn off the slow cooker. Leave to rest for 15 minutes. Serve with whipped topping and toffee bits.
**Per Serving:** Calories 170; Fat 7.9g; Sodium 204mg; Carbs 3g; Fiber 0g; Sugar 2g; Protein 19g

## Chocolate Nut Clusters

**Prep time: 15 minutes | Cook time: 2 hours 15 minutes | Serves: 60**

16 oz. dry-roasted peanuts, salted
16 oz. dry-roasted peanuts, unsalted
1 can (9.75 oz.) whole cashews, salted
36 oz. chocolate-flavored candy coating, chopped
12 oz. (2 cups) semisweet chocolate chips
1 bar (4 oz.) sweet baking chocolate, chopped
1 teaspoon vanilla extract

1. Spray a 3½- to slow cooker with cooking spray. in the slow cooker, mix all ingredients except cashews and vanilla extract. 2. Cover the slow cooker and cook on low-heat setting for 2 hours. 3. Line the necessary number of cookie sheets (depending on their size) with waxed paper. stir mixture in the slow cooker until smooth. 4. Add cashews and vanilla extract, stir until cashews are coated. Drop mixture by heaping tablespoon onto cookie sheets. Let stand until firm. 5. Store tightly covered at room temperature.
**Per Serving:** Calories 276; Fat 16g; Sodium 70mg; Carbs 1g; Fiber 0g; Sugar 0g; Protein 30g

## Bananas Foster

**Prep time: 10 minutes | Cook time: 1 hour 15 minutes | Serves: 7**

½ cup dark brown sugar
3 tablespoon butter, cut into pieces
¼ cup light unsweetened coconut milk
1 cup fresh pineapples, cubed
4 ripe bananas, cut into ½-inch-thick slices
1¾ cups vanilla reduced-fat ice cream
¼ teaspoon ground cinnamon
¼ cup dark rum

1. Grease a 3½-quart slow cooker with cooking spray. In the slow cooker, stir the brown sugar, butter, coconut milk and rum. 2. Cover the slow cooker and cook on low-heat setting for one hour. Whisking makes a smooth mixture. 3. Grease the pineapples, cinnamon and bananas in the sauce. 4. Cover the slow cooker and cook for 15 minutes longer. Serve warm with ice cream.
**Per Serving:** Calories 145; Fat 7.2g; Sodium 66mg; Carbs 7g; Fiber 2g; Sugar 2g; Protein 15g

## Carrot Walnut Cake

**Prep time: 15 minutes | Cook time: 2½ hours | Serves: 10**

2 cups whole-wheat flour
2 teaspoons baking powder
½ teaspoon baking soda
2 teaspoons ground cinnamon
½ teaspoon kosher salt
¾ cup packed light brown sugar
2 large eggs
½ cup vegetable oil, plus more for greasing
1 cup unsweetened almond milk
1 teaspoon pure vanilla extract
2 cups shredded carrots (about 4 medium carrots)
1 cup walnuts, chopped

1. In a bowl, whisk the flour, baking powder, baking soda, cinnamon, and salt. Stir in the brown sugar. 2. In a bowl, whisk the eggs, oil, milk, and vanilla. Add the egg mixture to the flour mixture and stir until well blended. Fold in the carrots and walnuts. The batter should be thick. 3. Grease a slow cooker with oil. Transfer the batter to the slow cooker. Make the outside edge thicker than the center because the center takes longer to cook. 4. Cover the slow cooker and cook on high temp setting for 2 to 2½ hours, or until a toothpick inserted between the center and the edge of the cake comes out clean. Serve warm. 5. Refrigerate leftovers for up to 1 week or freeze for up to 3 months.
**Per Serving:** Calories 629; Fat 61g; Sodium 64mg; Carbs 3g; Fiber 1g; Sugar 1g; Protein 18g

## Orange Apple Cider

**Prep time: 5 minutes | Cook time: 3 hours | Serves: 8**

½ gallon unsweetened apple cider or apple juice
1 teaspoon whole allspice
1 teaspoon whole cloves
10 (4-inch) cinnamon sticks, divided
1 orange, sliced
1 orange, cut into 8 wedges

1. In a slow cooker, combine the cider, allspice, cloves, and 2 cinnamon sticks. Float the orange slices on top. 2. Cover the slow cooker and cook on low temp setting for 2 to 3 hours, until the cider is heated through. 3. Remove the spices and orange slices with a slotted spoon. 4. Pour into mugs and garnish with the cinnamon sticks and orange wedges.
**Per Serving:** Calories 282; Fat 13.7g; Sodium 50mg; Carbs 4g; Fiber 0g; Sugar 1g; Protein 35g

## Pumpkin Cheesecake

**Prep time: 20 minutes | Cook time: 10 hours | Serves: 8**

**Cheesecake:**
2 packages (8 oz. each) cream cheese, softened
2 eggs
¾ cup sugar

**Crust:**
1¼ cups graham cracker crumbs
⅓ cup sugar

½ cup canned pumpkin
½ teaspoon pumpkin pie spice

¼ cup butter, melted

1. Apply some cooking spray on a spring form pan. 2. In a bowl, mix crust ingredients. Form the crust at the pan 1 inch up the sides. 3. In another bowl, using an electric mixer beat cream cheese just until smooth. 4. Lower the speed and gradually beat in ¾ cup sugar, and then beat in the eggs, one at a time, just until blended. 5. Spread three-fourths of the cream cheese mixture into the pan. Beat pumpkin and pumpkin pie spice into cream cheese mixture with whisk until smooth. Spoon over mixture in pan. 6. Place a small ovenproof bowl on a 6 or 7-quart round slow cooker (about 9 inches in diameter). Place a heatproof plate on top of the bowl. Set the cheesecake on the plate. 7. Place three layers of paper towels across the top of the slow cooker. Cover it with the lid to seal. 8. Cook on high- heat setting for 3 hours without removing the lid. Turn the slow cooker off and let stand, untouched, one hour. 9. Open the lid and remove paper towels. Transfer the cheesecake to the refrigerator. 10. Refrigerate before serving, not less 6 hours and no longer than 24 hours.
**Per Serving:** Calories 216; Fat 10.4g; Sodium 311mg; Carbs 14g; Fiber 1g; Sugar 2g; Protein 18g

## Delicious Peach Mango Crisp

Prep time: 10 minutes | Cook time: 6 hours | Serves: 12

½ cup vegetable oil, plus more for greasing
2 pounds frozen peach slices, partially thawed
1 pound frozen mango chunks, partially thawed
1 tablespoon freshly squeezed lemon juice
1 teaspoon pure vanilla extract or almond extract
½ cup whole-wheat flour
¼ teaspoon kosher salt
2 teaspoons ground cinnamon
1 teaspoon baking powder
¼ teaspoon baking soda
½ cup packed light brown sugar
1 cup rolled oats
⅔ cup sliced almonds
Whipped cream, for serving

1. Grease a slow cooker with oil. In the slow cooker, toss the peaches, mango, lemon juice, and vanilla. Spread the mixture into an even layer. 2. In a bowl, whisk the flour, salt, cinnamon, baking powder, and baking soda. Stir in the brown sugar, oats, and almonds. Add the oil and stir until well blended. Spread the flour mixture evenly over the peach mixture in the slow cooker. 3. Cover the slow cooker with a clean kitchen towel or paper towels. (Be careful to not let it drop in the middle. You don't want it touching the crisp.) Place the slow cooker lid on top of the towel. Cook on low temp setting for 5 to 6 hours, until hot and bubbly. 4. Remove the towel and serve with whipped cream.
**Per Serving:** Calories 227; Fat 11.2g; Sodium 412mg; Carbs 1g; Fiber 0g; Sugar 1g; Protein 31g

## Bread Pudding with Dried Fruits

Prep time: 15 minutes | Cook time: 3 hours | Serves: 10

Nonstick cooking spray or olive oil, for greasing
5 to 6 cups day-old whole-grain bread, crumbled or cubed
1 cup unsweetened dried fruit of choice
6 large eggs
4 cups 2% milk
½ cup packed light brown sugar
1 teaspoon pure vanilla extract
Whipped cream, for serving

1. Grease a slow cooker with nonstick spray or brush with oil. Evenly spread half of the bread in the slow cooker, followed by half of the fruit. Repeat the layers with the bread and fruit. 2. In a bowl, whisk the eggs, milk, brown sugar, and vanilla. 3. Pour the milk mixture over the bread and fruit in the slow cooker. 4. Push the bread down to make sure it is submerged. 5. Cover the slow cooker and cook on high temp setting for 2½ to 3 hours, until the liquid is absorbed and the bread pudding reaches an internal temperature of 190°F. 6. Spoon into serving bowls and top with whipped cream.
**Per Serving:** Calories 342; Fat 11.8g; Sodium 683mg; Carbs 24g; Fiber 4g; Sugar 1g; Protein 38g

# Conclusion

As the name implies, slow cookers are kitchen tools that take their time to prepare meals. In contrast to pressure cookers, they. An easy-to-use, portable electric device that is common in modern kitchens is the slow cooker. Slow cookers provide several benefits. "All day cooking without seeing" is what it is. They are inexpensive to run and an excellent technique to soften less costly and harder meat pieces (shoulder, round, and chuck). Foods have more taste when they are cooked slowly. One-pot dinners, soups, stews, and casseroles are just a few of the many dishes that may be prepared in a slow cooker. Compared to an oven, a slow cooker consumes less power.

# Appendix 1 Measurement Conversion Chart

## VOLUME EQUIVALENTS (LIQUID)

| US STANDARD | US STANDARD (OUNCES) | METRIC (APPROXIMATE) |
|---|---|---|
| 2 tablespoons | 1 fl.oz | 30 mL |
| ¼ cup | 2 fl.oz | 60 mL |
| ½ cup | 4 fl.oz | 120 mL |
| 1 cup | 8 fl.oz | 240 mL |
| 1½ cup | 12 fl.oz | 355 mL |
| 2 cups or 1 pint | 16 fl.oz | 475 mL |
| 4 cups or 1 quart | 32 fl.oz | 1 L |
| 1 gallon | 128 fl.oz | 4 L |

## VOLUME EQUIVALENTS (DRY)

| US STANDARD | METRIC (APPROXIMATE) |
|---|---|
| ⅛ teaspoon | 0.5 mL |
| ¼ teaspoon | 1 mL |
| ½ teaspoon | 2 mL |
| ¾ teaspoon | 4 mL |
| 1 teaspoon | 5 mL |
| 1 tablespoon | 15 mL |
| ¼ cup | 59 mL |
| ½ cup | 118 mL |
| ¾ cup | 177 mL |
| 1 cup | 235 mL |
| 2 cups | 475 mL |
| 3 cups | 700 mL |
| 4 cups | 1 L |

## TEMPERATURES EQUIVALENTS

| FAHRENHEIT (F) | CELSIUS (C) (APPROXIMATE) |
|---|---|
| 225 ℉ | 107℃ |
| 250 ℉ | 120℃ |
| 275 ℉ | 135℃ |
| 300 ℉ | 150℃ |
| 325 ℉ | 160℃ |
| 350 ℉ | 180℃ |
| 375 ℉ | 190℃ |
| 400 ℉ | 205℃ |
| 425 ℉ | 220℃ |
| 450 ℉ | 235℃ |
| 475 ℉ | 245℃ |
| 500 ℉ | 260℃ |

## WEIGHT EQUIVALENTS

| US STANDARD | METRIC (APPROXINATE) |
|---|---|
| 1 ounce | 28 g |
| 2 ounces | 57 g |
| 5 ounces | 142 g |
| 10 ounces | 284 g |
| 15 ounces | 425g |
| 16 ounces (1 pound) | 455 g |
| 1.5pounds | 680 g |
| 2pounds | 907g |

# Appendix 2 Recipes Index

## A

Apple and Granola Casserole 19
Aromatic Chicken Cacciatore 43
Avocado Sauce 71

## B

Bacon Cabbage Casserole 33
Baked Apples with Pecans 78
Bananas Foster 84
Barbecued Chicken 34
Beans Stuffed Sweet Potatoes 25
Beef & Butternut Squash Stew 67
Beef Bolognese 44
Beef Chili and Pinto Beans 50
Beef Meatballs with Tomatoes 45
Beef Pot Roast 47
Beef Roast with Vegetables 47
Beef with Bean Burrito Casserole 48
Beet & Spinach Frittata 14
Blueberry-Peach Oats Cobbler 78
Bread Pudding with Dried Fruits 86
Buffalo Cashews Dip 71

## C

Carrot Walnut Cake 84
Chai Latte 79
Cheese Veggie Frittata 15
Cheesy Artichoke and Spinach Sauce 73
Cheesy Buffalo Chicken Dip 74
Cheesy Cod with White Potatoes 56
Cheesy Flounder with Almonds 60
Cheesy Oatmeal with Spinach 16
Cheesy Omelet Casserole 18
Cheesy Potato Gratin 30
Cheesy Salmon with Root Vegetables 56
Cheesy Salsa Chicken 39
Cheesy Spring Vegetable Pasta 27
Chicken Chili with Beans 40
Chicken Noodle with Colorful Veggies 40
Chicken Strips with Tomatoes 37
Chicken Veggie Broth 34
Chicken-Apple Sausage 14
Chickpea and Carrots Soup 66
Chocolate Chip Lava Cake 80
Chocolate Nut Clusters 83
Chocolate-Toffee Lava Cake 83
Cinnamon Apple Pie Oats 15
Classic Beef Bones Broth 44
Classical Marinara Sauce 72
Coconut-Cacao Brownies 79
Coffee Pork Tacos 52
Collard Greens with Bacon 29
Cranberries Quinoa-Oat Cereal 20
Creamy Cashews Sauce 77
Creamy Cauliflower Soup 69
Creamy Pumpkin Steel-Cut Oats 21
Creamy Wild Rice Stew with Mushrooms 62
Creamy Zucchini Soup 67

## D

Dates Millet Porridge 20
Delicious BBQ Sauce 63
Delicious Beef Stroganoff 48
Delicious Bone Broth 66
Delicious Chicken Meatloaf 42
Delicious Peach Mango Crisp 86
Delicious Turkey Stuffed Peppers 32

## E

Easy Rustic Marinara Sauce 76
Easy Spaghetti Squash 25

## F

Fish and Vegetable Risotto 57

## G

Garlic, Spinach and Beans Chili 27
Garlic-Citrus Chicken with Potatoes 43
Garlicky Fish Stock 65
Garlicky Mashed Red Potatoes 33
Garlicky Turkey Breasts 41
Gingered Pork Chops with Carrots 46

## H

Hard-Boiled Eggs 13
Healthy Beans 26
Healthy Berry Oats Crumble 82
Healthy Butternut Squash Soup 62
Healthy Salsa Chicken 36
Healthy Salsa Verde Pork 53
Healthy Vegetable Frittata 22
Herbed Chicken and Cherry Tomatoes 42

...ed Chicken Barley Stew 64

Herbed Chicken with White Bean Stew 35

Herbed Greens with Onions 32

Herbed Meat Sauce 75

Herbed Pork Loin with Dried Fruit and Leeks 49

Herbed Root Vegetable Hash 17

Herbed Split Pea and Carrot Soup 61

Hot Coconut Cereal 19

## I

Italian Chicken with Spaghetti Soup 70

Italian-style Bolognese Sauce 76

## L

Lemon Chickpea Soup 69

Lemony Salmon with Zucchini and Carrot 57

## M

Mashed Root Vegetables 28

Mixed Berries Butter Toast 16

Moroccan-style Lamb Shanks 46

Multi-Grain Granola with Cherries 18

## N

Nutty Apple-Peach Crumble 81

Nutty Granola with Dried Berries 22

## O

Onion & Bell Pepper Stuffed Tomatoes 29

Orange Apple Cider 85

## P

Peachy Brown Betty with Cranberries 82

Peppercorn Chicken Stock 64

Pesto Cod with White Bean Ratatouille 59

Pork and Celery with Mulled Cider 51

Pork and Pumpkin Stew 45

Pork Loin Roast with Potatoes 50

Protein Soup 63

Pulled Pork with Juicy Pineapple 51

Pumpkin Cheesecake 85

Roasted butternut Squash Purée 31

## R

Roasted Fennel Chicken and Squash 38

Roasted Vegetables 30

## S

Saucy Bolognese Sauce 72

Shrimp and Scallop Tacos 55

Shrimp with Cheesy Grits 59

Shrimp with Corn Chowder 58

Southwest Chicken with Zucchini 39

Spiced Smoky Barbecue Sauce 74

Spicy Chicken Tortilla Soup 68

Spicy Chicken with Greens 38

Spicy Eggs in Purgatory 17

Spicy Monkfish with Sweet Potatoes 58

Spicy Whole Chicken 35

Spinach Ham Quiche 23

Stewed Fruit with Herbs 80

Stuffed Peppers with Ground Beef and Rice 49

Sweet & Sour Beets with Onions 31

Sweet & Spicy Turkey Salad 41

Sweet Garlic Chicken and Carrots 37

Sweet Pork Tenderloin with Pomegranate Seeds 54

Sweet Potato & Onion Casserole 13

## T

Tangy Apple Cider Wassail 81

Tangy Cinnamon-Berry Sauce 75

Tangy Sweet Potato and Leek Soup 61

Tangy Teriyaki Beef 53

Thai Chicken Curry 36

Tomato Sauce 73

Tropical Farro with Mango and Nuts 21

Tropical Thai-Style Curry Pork Tenderloin 52

Trout with Carrot Mélange 55

Turkey & Spinach Soup 68

## U

Udon Noodle Soup with Veggie 28

## V

Vegan Navy Beans with Cranberries 26

Vegetable Broth 24

Veggie and Quinoa Casserole 24

## W

Wild Rice with Vegetable Soup 65

Printed in Great Britain
by Amazon